CAESAR

There are a number of HORIZON CARAVEL BOOKS
published each year. Titles now available are:

BUILDING THE SUEZ CANAL
MOUNTAIN CONQUEST
PHARAOHS OF EGYPT
LEONARDO DA VINCI
THE FRENCH REVOLUTION
CORTES AND THE AZTEC CONQUEST
CAESAR
THE UNIVERSE OF GALILEO AND NEWTON
THE VIKINGS
MARCO POLO'S ADVENTURES IN CHINA

SHAKESPEARE'S ENGLAND
CAPTAIN COOK AND THE SOUTH PACIFIC
THE SEARCH FOR EARLY MAN
JOAN OF ARC
EXPLORATION OF AFRICA
NELSON AND THE AGE OF FIGHTING SAIL
ALEXANDER THE GREAT
RUSSIA UNDER THE CZARS
HEROES OF POLAR EXPLORATION
KNIGHTS OF THE CRUSADES

American Heritage also publishes AMERICAN HERITAGE JUNIOR LIBRARY
books, a similar series on American history. The titles now available are:

CAPTAINS OF INDUSTRY
CARRIER WAR IN THE PACIFIC
JAMESTOWN: FIRST ENGLISH COLONY
AMERICANS IN SPACE
ABRAHAM LINCOLN IN PEACE AND WAR
AIR WAR AGAINST HITLER'S GERMANY
IRONCLADS OF THE CIVIL WAR
THE ERIE CANAL
THE MANY WORLDS OF BENJAMIN FRANKLIN
COMMODORE PERRY IN JAPAN
THE BATTLE OF GETTYSBURG
ANDREW JACKSON, SOLDIER AND STATESMAN
ADVENTURES IN THE WILDERNESS
LEXINGTON, CONCORD AND BUNKER HILL
CLIPPER SHIPS AND CAPTAINS
D-DAY, THE INVASION OF EUROPE

WESTWARD ON THE OREGON TRAIL
THE FRENCH AND INDIAN WARS
GREAT DAYS OF THE CIRCUS
STEAMBOATS ON THE MISSISSIPPI
COWBOYS AND CATTLE COUNTRY
TEXAS AND THE WAR WITH MEXICO
THE PILGRIMS AND PLYMOUTH COLONY
THE CALIFORNIA GOLD RUSH
PIRATES OF THE SPANISH MAIN
TRAPPERS AND MOUNTAIN MEN
MEN OF SCIENCE AND INVENTION
NAVAL BATTLES AND HEROES
THOMAS JEFFERSON AND HIS WORLD
DISCOVERERS OF THE NEW WORLD
RAILROADS IN THE DAYS OF STEAM
INDIANS OF THE PLAINS

THE STORY OF YANKEE WHALING

A HORIZON CARAVEL BOOK

CAESAR

By the Editors of
HORIZON MAGAZINE

Author
IRWIN ISENBERG

Consultant
RICHARD M. HAYWOOD
Professor of Classics, New York University

ILLUSTRATED WITH SCULPTURE, MOSAICS,
AND ARTIFACTS OF THE PERIOD

Published by American Heritage Publishing Co., Inc.
Book Trade and Institutional Distribution by
Harper & Row

SECOND PRINTING

Library of Congress Catalogue Card Number: 64–22872
© 1964 by American Heritage Publishing Co., Inc., 551 Fifth Avenue, New York 17,
New York. All rights reserved under Berne and Pan-American Copyright Conventions.
Trademark CARAVEL registered United States Patent Office

FOREWORD

In larger quantities than most young men, Gaius Julius Caesar had brains, courage, and helpful family ties, but there were few signs that he would use them. Then suddenly, between the years 60 and 44 B.C., when he was in his forties and fifties, he began to excel in everything he attempted. As an orator and politician, as a general, a writer, and a statesman he stood above all men of his day. With an unerring sense of timing and tactics, he devoted himself to one supreme task: the transformation of Rome from a powerful but small republic into a world empire with himself at its head. On the point of achieving this goal, he was stabbed by a score of knives in the hall of the Roman Senate, assassinated by reactionaries who could not endure to have their

Julius Caesar's triumphal procession into Rome in 45 B.C. is pictured in this richly colored painting by the Renaissan

world so totally changed. They killed the man, but not the power of his name.

Such a heroic tale, brimming with battles, triumphs, and intrigue, could hardly have escaped the notice of artists in Caesar's own day and in the twenty subsequent centuries. This book brings together the facts and the myths of Caesar's life with pertinent art, documents, and photographs and reconstructions of significant sites. The portraits of Caesar range from realistic, contemporary likenesses to portrayals of him as a Renaissance prince (below). Each new age tended to represent him as one of its own.

But, curiously, there are no recent works showing this extraordinary man either in battle or enthroned in majesty. Heroism, on the magnificent scale of Caesar, went out of fashion with the coming of the modern world and may indeed never return. As Mark Antony remarked in Shakespeare's *Julius Caesar*, "O! What a fall was there, my countrymen . . ."

THE EDITORS

rtist Paolo Uccello. Preceding Caesar's throne (far left) is a cart decorated with the helmets of the prisoners inside.

This is the most famous portrait of Caesar, a marble bust made not long after his assassination.
MUSEO NAZIONALE, NAPLES: ALINARI

COVER: A life-like and life-size statue of Caesar is posed against a background of aristocratic purple.
CAPITOLINE MUSEUM, ROME: EMMETT BRIGHT

FRONT ENDSHEET: Roman politicians arranged entertainments like this chariot race to win popularity.
MUSEO ARQUEOLOGICO, BARCELONA: PHOTO MAS.

TITLE PAGE: Two wretched prisoners sit huddled under their captured arms on a coin of Caesar's.
BIBLIOTHEQUE NATIONALE, CABINET DES MEDAILLES: SERVICE PHOTOGRAPHIQUE

BACK ENDSHEET: In a scene from a column in Rome, soldiers drive captured men and beasts to market.
ANTONINE COLUMN, ROME: ALINARI

BACK COVER: A gold frame set with gems makes a rich setting for this antique cameo head of Caesar.
BIBLIOTHEQUE NATIONALE, CABINET DES MEDAILLES: SERVICE PHOTOGRAPHIQUE

CONTENTS

FOREWORD 6

I   A YOUNG ARISTOCRAT 10

II   THE ROAD TO POWER 28

III   THE TRIUMVIRATE 44

IV   GENERAL FOR THE LEGIONS 60

V   CAMPAIGN OF CONQUEST 78

VI   ACROSS THE RUBICON 100

VII   HAIL, CAESAR! 118

VIII   THE IDES OF MARCH 136

ACKNOWLEDGMENTS 150

FURTHER REFERENCE 151

INDEX 152

Caesar's mythical ancestor, Venus, is seen at left in this wall painting from Pompeii. Dressed as a Roman matron, she is seated before the war god Mars.

I

A YOUNG ARISTOCRAT

Centuries after his death, Caesar still seemed so super-human that men found it hard to believe he had been born in the normal manner. The legend grew that he had been pulled forth from an incision in his mother's body—which is how the surgical term Caesarean originated.

History, however, gives the legend no support. It merely records that he was born about 100 B.C. to the aristocratic Julian family, which proudly traced its ancestry back to the goddess Venus. He was called Gaius Julius Caesar, as his father and grandfather had been before him. For according to custom, the eldest son of a Roman family was usually named after his father and had three names altogether: his personal name (in this case Gaius), the name of his family's clan (Julius), and the surname, or family name (Caesar). Surnames were often nicknames—Caesar's family name meant "hairy."

But the birth of this proudly named child was overshadowed by news of the exploits of another member of the family, Gaius Marius, who was married to the young Caesar's aunt, Julia.

Marius himself had sprung from plebeian, or common, stock; his father was a farmer from a small village some sixty miles from Rome. As a young man Marius had plunged into politics, one of the roughest careers for a commoner to follow in that undemocratic age. For the aristocrats—the patricians—had a tight grip on the government; they despised the "new men," as they scornfully called the plebeian politicians, and fought to keep them out of power.

Marius was a tough, burly fellow, both physically and mentally, and he quickly won the loyalty of the common people. He defied the aristocratic Senate when it tried to curtail the voting rights of the plebeians, and before long,

Gaius Marius, strikingly portrayed in this bust of about 30 B.C., was a great general but a poor statesman. His rashness almost destroyed the popular party he had established.

he had made a name for himself as the champion of the people. But ability and drive and popularity were not enough for a commoner who wanted to get to the top. He needed an ally among the patricians. Marius found one in the Julian family, and he sealed the alliance by marrying Caesar's aunt. The Julians were delighted to have this rising politician in the family, even though he was a plebeian. And Marius now had the prestige of the Julian name, along with the votes they controlled, to back his bid for power. He was elected consul in 108 B.C.

Once in office, he showed his talents in another field, for he proved to be a brilliant general. He persuaded the Senate to send him to Africa to replace Quintus Metellus, who had led a Roman army there to put down an uprising led by the rebellious king of Numidia. Marius' move was an act of treachery, since Metellus' family had sponsored him at the start of his career, and he had served under Metellus before becoming consul. But loyalty meant nothing to Marius in his drive for power.

Lucius Cornelius Sulla composed his own epitaph. In it he characterized himself aptly as a man who always repaid in full the kindness of his friends and the hatred of his foes.

In Africa he soon brought an end to the fighting, which had been dragging on for years. However, the honor of capturing the rebel king fell to Lucius Sulla, the commander of the Roman cavalry. Marius never forgave Sulla for this, and a bitter enmity grew up between the two men, an enmity that finally plunged Rome into a bloody civil war. For the moment, however, Marius was on top of the world.

He returned to Rome in triumph to find another opportunity for fame awaiting him. Wandering German tribes had invaded the north of Italy, defeating two Roman armies that had been sent against them. The city of Rome was in grave danger; moreover, Roman pride had been offended. The people looked to Marius to avenge them. He took to the field once again, and in the years just prior to his nephew's birth, he defeated the invaders and drove them from Roman soil.

The figure of Marius the warrior and champion of the people must have loomed large over his nephew's early

TEXT CONTINUED ON PAGE 16

THE FORUM, PAST AND PRESENT

Little of the Forum remains today, as the photograph at right attests. Even less of the Forum of Caesar's youth (plan above) remains, for he and his successors rebuilt it. In the foreground (1 on the plan) is the Temple of Castor and Pollux with three columns still standing. To its right is the paved area of the Forum itself, and to its left is the site of the multistoried market, the Basilica Julia, built by Caesar to replace the smaller Basilica Sempronia (2), which had stood there in his childhood. Pictured below is a scene in the arcade of a basilica, with shoppers bargaining over the wares spread out on the floor. Behind the basilica are the ruins of the Temple of Saturn, the Roman treasury (3), with some columns intact; in the photograph's background is the red wall of the Tabularium, or archives (4). In front of the Tabularium is the Temple of Concord (5)—now a grassy plot. The Curia, or Senate house (6), stood to the right—out of the photograph—with the Rostra, or speaker's platform (7), in its courtyard. To the southeast of them was another market, the Basilica Aemilia (8). On the near side of the Via Sacra, the cobbled road running diagonally across the picture, was the High Priest's residence (9), the House of the Vestals (10), and the Temple of Vesta (11). These were located in front of the ruined wall in the lower right corner of the photograph. Both plan and photograph face northwest, as indicated by the arrow with the initials SPQR—standing for "the Senate and People of Rome."

Little of the Rome Caesar knew remained in the fourteenth century, when the map above was made. Yet the city's area had not radically changed, and some of the classical buildings still stood, notably the Coliseum (domed edifice below center). But the Forum had become a pasture called the Cow Field.

TEXT CONTINUED FROM PAGE 13

years. Certainly young Caesar learned many lessons from Marius' career. However, as a patrician, he had numerous advantages that Marius had missed, including a first-class education. Like all young patrician men, he was trained for a life in politics, and he studied the subjects that would best fit him for his work: Greek and Latin literature, philosophy, and most important of all, rhetoric, the art of persuasive argument, for which he showed a natural talent.

Gaius Julius Caesar was also introduced to politics by listening to the conversation of his elders as they discussed the latest happenings in the Senate—for most of the men of his family were senators or held political offices—or talked of the news that arrived daily from all parts of the Roman state and its provinces. When the boy reached the age of twelve, he was taken to the Curia, or Senate house, to hear the speeches and debates and watch the statesmen at work.

The Curia stood at the northeast corner of the Roman Forum, which was the heart of Rome. The Forum was an open, stone-paved area, two hundred yards long and seventy yards wide, where Romans had gathered from the earliest days to debate their affairs, to hold their courts, and to vote. On the east side, in front of the Curia, was a high platform from which speakers could address the crowds. It was called the Rostra, from the rams (*rostra*) of captured enemy warships that were fastened to the front of it. Opposite the Rostra, on the other side of the Forum, was a huge two-storied indoor market, the Basilica Sempronia, and to the west of that was the Temple of Saturn, which housed the state treasury and the offices of the quaestors, or treasury masters.

One building that young Caesar must have known well was the Regia, the offices of the High Priest, at the eastern end of the Forum. Here he could usually find his uncle, Caius Cotta, who held an important position in the College of Priests. The Regia stood in a group of religious buildings that also included the Temple of Vesta (goddess of the hearth and household), the House of the Vestals (priestesses who served in the temple), and the Temple of Castor and Pollux, which was a favorite meeting place for merchants and other wealthy citizens.

Yet another temple stood at the opposite end of the Forum—the Temple of Concord, one of the oldest in

As a mark of his freeborn status, the young patrician at left wears a locket on a cord around his neck. His toga is purple-bordered, like a senator's, to show that even a well-born child should be treated with respect. But the patrician scholar at right above, who has arrived late, receives no respect from his angry schoolmaster.

17

Rome. Behind that was the Tabularium, where the state records were stored. The whole area around the Forum was in fact crowded with official buildings and temples, with small stores, booths, and workshops filling the spaces between them. All day long the Forum was a busy and noisy place alive with a bustle of people hurrying about their business and with throngs of others, less busy, who gathered on the steps of the buildings or along the arcades to while away the hours talking and gambling.

This lively scene was a familiar sight to Caesar as he grew to manhood. But he also knew a less cheerful Forum, one emptied of people by the periods of violence that marked his early years. And no one was more to blame for these times of strife and bloodshed than his uncle, Marius.

The last phase of Marius' career began when he left Rome after quarreling with other popular-party leaders. He was recalled from this self-imposed exile in 91 B.C. to lead a Roman army once again—this time against a new enemy, the Italian cities. These cities had become part of the Roman state during the previous centuries when Rome was bringing the Italian peninsula under her control. Al-

By usury, and by their strangle-hold on food imports, the middle classes weakened Rome's economy. Above at center, a typical banker receives interest payments from four bearded farmers, and below, at far left, the owner of a grain ship watches as his cargo is loaded.

though the Italian peoples were considered citizens of the republic in most respects, they had been denied the right to vote in the elections at Rome. Now they rebelled in the hope of forcing the Romans to give them that right.

In the Social Wars, as the revolt was called, Marius led his troops with customary skill, even though he was now seventy years old. But the credit for the victory, which came in 88 B.C., went to his rival Sulla, who had shown himself to be as capable a general as his former commander. This only added fuel to Marius' hatred; he felt that he had been cheated once again. But worse was to follow.

The end of the rebellion brought no peace to Rome. There was trouble in her Greek provinces, which had been invaded by the armies of Mithridates, ruler of Pontus, a kingdom on the Black Sea coast of Asia Minor. Mithridates ordered his allies in the Greek provinces to massacre the Roman citizens who still remained there, and thousands were put to the sword. So with one war hardly over, Rome had to prepare for another.

Marius, Rome's greatest general and still a popular hero, expected to lead the army, but many thought him too old; besides, his mind was becoming dim with alcohol. So the Senate passed him over in favor of Sulla. At once Marius' friends pushed an act through the People's Assembly which took the command away from Sulla and gave it to the old man. Sulla was undeterred—he had little time for legalities, and even less for Marius and his friends. He hurried to his camp outside Rome, and with his six legions at his back, marched on the city. Marius and his party

The second-century astronomer Ptolemy was the first to write a scientific work on geography. This map, from an early printed edition of his treatise, shows the lands around the Mediterranean, many of which became part of the Roman Empire.

were expelled, but the war with Mithridates would not wait. Sulla could not linger in Rome to make sure of his victory. He had to sail for Greece almost immediately.

No sooner was he out of the way than Marius and Cinna, his most powerful colleague, appeared at the head of a mob of brigands and freed slaves and massacred Sulla's followers in the streets of Rome. Then the two men had themselves elected consuls for 86 B.C. But Marius was cheated again; he died just a few days after the elections, leaving Cinna to rule alone.

Cinna did not have much longer to live either. By the following year, Sulla had forced Mithridates to come to terms and was ready to return to Rome. Cinna raised an army to meet him and was preparing to ship his troops to Greece when a riot broke out in their camp and he was killed in the fighting. Marius' party was now leaderless

Although Mithridates (above) challenged the Romans for twenty-seven years, they gave him a royal burial.

and could not prevent Sulla's followers from seizing control of the government. Sulla entered Rome in triumph and quickly set about hunting down his enemies. It was said that three thousand of them died in the blood bath that followed; certainly, few of the popular party escaped. But among those few was young Gaius Julius Caesar, who found himself pitched headlong into politics.

Caesar was in double danger. Not only was he Marius' nephew, but he had also married Cinna's daughter, Cornelia, just a short time before. Still, despite his training and his uncle's influence, he had never shown any real interest in politics. He was known as a ladies' man and a dandy who was more interested in the draping of his toga than in the fate of Rome. His marriage had been made by his family as a business arrangement, as most patrician marriages were. And his only contact with public life had been his appointment to the post of priest of Jupiter, which had also been arranged by his family.

Sulla, to test Caesar's loyalty, ordered him to divorce Cornelia. Most men would have thought it wise to obey such a command, but Caesar—whether through love for his wife or through hatred of Sulla—refused and placed himself in mortal danger.

Believing that Sulla would order his execution despite his innocence, Caesar fled from Rome and took refuge in the hilly country to the northeast of the city. But there was little safety anywhere. Sulla's men were hunting down fugitives all through the countryside.

For some weeks, Caesar with a small band of his slaves managed to elude the hunters. Then he fell ill, exhausted by night marches and sleeping on the ground, and he had to be carried on a stretcher. Moving after dark, the slaves bore him from one hiding place to another. One night they were surprised by a patrol, but Caesar bribed the captain to let him go, and the miserable flight continued.

Weary and without hope, Caesar thought of quitting Italy altogether and going into exile. But before he could take any action, he received word that powerful friends in Rome were trying to obtain a pardon for him. So he returned to the city, where his wife nursed him back to health.

At last the day arrived when he had to face Sulla. He set out with his friends through the familiar streets to the Forum, where Sulla waited, seated on the Rostra. Caesar's friends went forward to plead his case. He was still only a boy, they argued; he was hotheaded, and his refusal to divorce his wife had nothing to do with politics.

Caesar's life hung in the balance; a single gesture from Sulla could mean his death. But when the dictator's hands moved, it was in a signal of pardon, and as the Roman historian Suetonius reports, Sulla said, "You have made your point, and you can have him, but always bear in mind that . . . one Caesar is worse than a dozen Mariuses."

Even with a pardon, Caesar saw that he was not safe in Rome. There was nothing to keep him there because Sulla had stripped him of his nomination to the priesthood. In 81 B.C., his chance came to leave. The proconsul Minucius Thermus was setting out for Asia Minor to deal with the rebellious Mytileneans, who had allied themselves with Mithridates in the recent war. Caesar was offered a post on Thermus' staff, and he went gladly.

Soon after his arrival in Asia Minor, he was sent on an important mission to Nicomedes, king of Bithynia on the Black Sea. Nicomedes was a staunch ally of Rome and had promised to lend his powerful fleet to Thermus for the blockade of the Mytileneans' chief city. But the fleet had not yet arrived. Caesar's job was to make sure that Nicomedes did not go back on his promise.

The luxury of Nicomedes' court overwhelmed the young Roman, for the king made a lavish show of his wealth. On his first night in Bithynia, Caesar slept in a bed of gold, and on the following day he was the guest of honor at a royal banquet. His head was turned by the display, and forgetting his position as the representative of Roman might, he acted as the king's cupbearer. This shocked some Roman merchants who were at the feast, for it was beneath the dignity of a Roman officer to behave that way. And his reputation was not improved when the tale got back to Rome. But, in the meantime, Caesar and Nicomedes became close friends, and the king showered gifts of money on the young man, whom he came to admire. Even so, Caesar did not forget the purpose of his visit; the fleet was sent to Thermus' aid.

Soon after, Caesar had to return to his duties with the army, although he must have done so reluctantly. However, he played his part in the successful campaign that followed. The city of Mytilene was taken by storm, and in the action, Caesar won the civic crown, Rome's highest award for courage. Then for a time, he was kept busy with administrative duties in Asia Minor until another opportunity for action presented itself. An expedition was being launched against the pirates in the eastern Mediterranean. Caesar offered his services, but before he could take up his

At the siege of Mytilene, Caesar won his first military award, the civic crown of oak leaves (above).

The orator at right, text in hand and gesturing dramatically, was a common sight in Rome, where oratory was a high art. Roman statesmen had to be polished speechmakers, and they spent years learning their craft. As an orator, Caesar was regarded as second only to Cicero, whom many hold to be the greatest.

MVNIFICENTIA.PII.SEXTI.P.M

23

new military post, news arrived from Rome that sent him hurrying back there. Sulla was dead.

Caesar was now twenty-two years old and at last ready to begin his political career. But after his joyous reunion with his wife and baby daughter, he found that the situation in Rome was not at all clear. Sulla's aristocratic forces were still strong, while Marius' old popular party was split by quarrels. Caesar refused to ally himself with either side, and for the moment seemed content to retire to private life. He wrote poetry, dabbled in the sciences, and gave lavish and expensive parties that plunged him deep into debt. However, creditors were easy to find; the moneylenders considered Caesar an up-and-coming young man who before long would be in a position to repay his debts many times over.

Despite this seemingly idle life, Caesar still nursed his ambitions. Even without taking sides, there was one way open for a young man to make a name for himself: he could defend or prosecute an official who had committed crimes while in office. Caesar chose as his victim one of Sulla's men, Gnaeus Dolabella, who had shocked even his own friends by his greedy plundering of public funds while governor of Macedonia. Caesar's speech of accusation was carefully prepared and made a good impression on the judges; nonetheless, Caesar lost the case. Dolabella had hired two of the best lawyers in Rome to defend him, and Caesar had little chance against their combined skills. In the following year, some Greek citizens brought another of Sulla's men to trial for looting their towns during the campaign against Mithridates. They hired Caesar to handle their case. This time he was a little more successful; the accused man was found guilty, although the verdict was later set aside when he appealed.

Caesar's career was frustrated once again, it seemed. Besides, he had made some powerful enemies among Sulla's patrician party, and his debts were mounting. He decided to leave Rome for a while, and he took ship for the East.

His vessel was nearing the coast of Asia Minor when it was attacked by pirates who overwhelmed Caesar's party and made him a prisoner. As was their custom, they de-

When Caesar first joined a Roman battle action at Mytilene, the Roman army had already become the master of siege warfare. It kept this technological advantage until the fourth century, when this siege mosaic was made.

The pirates who haunted the eastern end of the Mediterranean in their swift galleys (right) plagued Rome for centuries. Their favorite victims were clumsy merchant ships like those above moving out to sea past the lighthouse at Alexandria.

manded a ransom—twenty talents (about thirty thousand dollars)—but Caesar scornfully told them he was worth more. He demanded that they set a price of fifty talents, which the pirates were happy to do. Caesar's companions set off at once to raise the money.

The Greek writer Plutarch, who records this story in his biography of Caesar, calls these pirates "a set of the most bloodthirsty people in the world." Caesar was their captive for thirty-eight days, but during this time, as Plutarch relates, he acted as though the pirates were his bodyguards rather than his captors. "He wrote verses and speeches and made [the pirates] his auditors, and those who did not admire them, he called to their faces illiterate and barbarous and would often . . . threaten to hang them. They were greatly taken with this and attributed his free talking to a kind of simplicity and boyish playfulness."

In this they were badly mistaken. When the ransom arrived, Caesar hurried off to raise a force of men from the nearby towns, offering them as pay all the booty they could take, including the fifty talents ransom money. His quick action caught the pirates unaware, and they were all apprehended. Caesar could not wait for the local officials to decide their fate, but carried out the threat he had made while a prisoner and hanged the brigands on the spot.

After this adventure, Caesar continued to the island of Rhodes to study rhetoric with the famous teacher Apollonius Molon. He had not been there long, however, when he heard that Mithridates had broken his treaty with Rome and was on the move again. Heading at once for Asia to raise troops at his own expense, Caesar fought a successful skirmish with the advance guard of Mithridates' army, which was probing into Roman territories. Soon after, a regularly appointed Roman general arrived to take charge of the war, and Caesar enrolled his little force in the army.

However, before the campaign could get under way, Caesar received a letter telling him that his mother's brother Cotta, the priest, had died and that the vacant seat in the College of Priests was being held for Caesar. This was an important post, unlike his earlier nomination, for it could lead to the office of High Priest of Rome.

So in 74 B.C., Caesar, now twenty-six years old, found himself taking ship for Rome for the third time to pick up the threads of his career.

THE ROAD TO POWER

The Rome to which Caesar returned in 74 B.C. was the mistress of the Mediterranean and the political heart of the lands around her shores. Many of these lands were already Roman provinces—Italy, Sicily, Macedonia, Greece, and parts of Spain and North Africa—while most of the kingdoms of the eastern Mediterranean looked to Rome as their protector and overlord. But this collection of territories was not yet an empire; it had been acquired piecemeal in the preceding centuries as Rome fought off and conquered one aggressor after another in a battle for survival. Yet already in Caesar's time, the Romans were laying the foundations of the empire that was to be the work of Caesar's successors. And already, Romans were beginning to enjoy the riches of the provinces. In 167 B.C. a law was passed that freed all Romans from paying taxes, since the treasury could be filled by the tribute from their subject states.

Vast private fortunes were also to be made in the provinces. Governors and generals lined their pockets with public funds. Financiers speculated in trade and made handsome profits on mortgages. Others lent money at high rates of interest to local rulers ruined by wars with Rome. Merchants grew wealthy importing the wine and olives of Greece and the metals of Asia. Others amassed fortunes by leasing from the Senate the right to collect taxes.

This new wealth brought an era of luxury to Rome such as had never been known before. And the rich—patricians and plebeians alike—loved to flaunt their money. They replaced the simple homes of their ancestors with magnificent palaces in the city, huge country estates, and villas

Wealthy Romans enjoyed giving sumptuous banquets (painting at right) at which slaves served wine (center) and removed the guests' shoes (left). Above, another slave pours wine from a jar marked ZHCHC, "long life" in Greek.

scattered along the coasts of Italy to which they could escape in the hot summers. Others founded large farms where they experimented with vines and new methods of agriculture and cattle breeding.

They used their wealth to furnish these mansions in a lavish manner. The most skillful painters and stonecarvers were hired to decorate the walls of the rooms. The finest works of sculpture were scattered in and around the houses, which were surrounded by magnificent gardens. Furniture was made of ivory and rare woods and enriched with ornate carvings and inlaid with precious metals.

They also spent huge sums entertaining friends and political allies. They gave long-drawn-out feasts at which the diners were entertained by dancers, acrobats, and musicians while they sipped rare wines and sampled exotic dishes—nightingales' tongues, peacocks, and mice cooked in honey.

There was plenty of time for the rich to indulge their taste for politics because slaves took care of most of their needs and much of their work. A wealthy man was followed by a train of slaves wherever he went. Slaves worked his farms and ran his house, cooked his meals, and raised and educated his children. His secretaries, librarians, and even his doctor were slaves. Some of them became trusted friends and confidantes of leading Roman citizens, but most slaves led a miserable existence. From time to time they rose in rebellion. In the year after Caesar's return from Asia, a Thracian gladiator named Spartacus banded together a force of slaves and filled Italy with terror until he was defeated by the Roman army.

Slaves were brought to Rome from all parts of the known world. They came as prisoners of war or were sold by pirates. Some had once been freemen but had been sold into slavery to pay their debts.

Most Romans, of course, could not afford slaves. Shopkeepers, craftsmen, and small merchants might have a slave or two, but the majority of the population was almost as wretched as the slaves themselves. They lived crowded into rickety tenements that lined the narrow streets. Their meals were no banquets. For the most part they ate bread and olives and a kind of porridge made of wheat with per-

MUSEO NAZIONALE, NAPLES: ALINARI

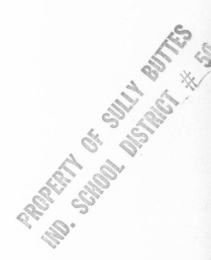

TEXT CONTINUED ON PAGE 34

Many rich Romans owned country houses similar to the first-century villa at left with its tree-shaded garden and its patron deity on a column. They furnished their rooms luxuriously with items such as the bronze table above.

31

The rooms of larger Roman houses were decorated with vivid murals, often copied from stage sets. At left is one corner of the bedroom of a house built about 50 B.C. The right-hand panel shows a luxurious mansion. Its imposing gates with their lion-headed silver handles are hung on pillars of imported marble. Behind the gates rises a cluster of buildings, one of which has a sun porch (center). The columned court of a house containing a small circular temple appears in the central panel, and a garden with a fountain and a vine-draped porch is at left.

33

This gladiator is a retiarius, *or "net-man." He tried to ensnare his opponents, who were heavily armored swordsmen, in a weighted net before killing them with his trident. Gladiators were not always entertainers; many politicians employed them as assassins and bodyguards.*

TEXT CONTINUED FROM PAGE 31

haps a few vegetables mixed in; meat was only available on special days or when a politician, looking for votes, gave a public feast.

But if the poor could not share the luxuries of the wealthy, they could always look forward to the games, which were held at the state's expense on certain holidays.

On the day of the games, the people would pour from their crowded tenements through the narrow streets and into the sun-bathed arena. When the spectators had filled the tiers of stone benches, the blare of a band would announce the entry into the stadium of the presiding dignitary, usually a consul or praetor. This was followed by a procession of priests and incense bearers carrying images of the gods and goddesses in whose honor the games were being held. Then the president of the games would give the signal for them to begin.

Sometimes the games consisted of chariot races. The chariots were drawn by two or four horses. Their drivers, the reins wrapped tightly round their waists to hold them steady, stood on a narrow step in the light two-wheeled carts. When the president raised his hand, the race was on. The chariots hurtled down the length of the arena, made a perilous turn around a column at the end, and then shot back up the other side. Seven times in all they rocketed around the course while the crowd cheered on their favorites and bet on the outcome. And there was always the added thrill of a spectacular crash and spill as wheels locked together with a shower of sparks on the tight turns.

Chariot racing was an exciting and dangerous sport, but there was another sport that the Roman mob loved better—the gladiatorial games. The gladiators were usually slaves or condemned criminals who were trained in the use of weapons in special schools. Their trainer was called, appropriately, the *lanista*, which was an ancient word for butcher. In the arena, the gladiators fought sometimes in teams but more often in single combat. Each was armed in a different way. Some of them had swords or daggers and shields; some had nets and tridents; some wore armor; some had none. But the same end awaited all—death on the sandy floor of the arena.

The fights began with a display of skill in which wooden weapons were used, but wooden blades were soon exchanged for steel, and the bloody work began. The crowd roared for their favorites and jeered at timid gladiators who were driven into the fight with whips. Wounded men fell, raising their forefingers to plead for mercy, which was given or withheld at the whim of the president. The victors accepted their palm branches, their only reward, and left

A Roman charioteer urges his four-horse team in pursuit of a rival who has beaten him around the last turn, marked by the carved columns at right, and is thundering along the stretch toward the finish line.

35

At left, in a first-century fresco, while gladiators battle inside the arena and excited spectators come to blows outside (far left), traders calmly carry on their business in their canvas stalls (at bottom).

Roman officials who presided at public occasions dressed and comported themselves with elaborate dignity. At right, Pompey the Great presides over the Senate.

the arena to nurse their wounds and to wait for the next games and another chance for glory or death.

These barbaric entertainments seem out of keeping with the sense of dignity and the love of law and order that marked Roman civilization. However, they were the entertainments of the common people, not of the aristocrats who ruled Rome. These patrician families held themselves aloof from the games for the most part, although they were not above using them as a means of winning votes. Any politician who put on a good show at his own expense could always rely on the people's gratitude at election time.

So far, Caesar had had no opportunity for gaining popularity in this way. In fact, he did not have the money, for he still had more debts than he could pay. However, his career seemed to be off to a good start at last. Shortly after his appointment to the College of Priests, he was also elected one of the six people's military tribunes. This office carried a small command in time of war and was not very important, but it was the first step on the ladder of office.

His two official positions brought Caesar into contact with all sorts of people. Many of them saw him in the Forum, where he spent most of the day carrying out his business. Others stopped him on the streets to ask for his help or to beg a favor, while the first part of every day was set aside for receiving callers at his house. And to everyone who sought him out, he showed courtesy and attention.

Already he was displaying a political astuteness that was uncommon in a young man. He never let slip an opportunity to increase his popularity or to keep himself in the public eye. As the Italian historian Guglielmo Ferrero wrote:

He kept a pleasantry or a compliment or a promise ready on his lips for all comers, invited necessary acquaintances to dinner every evening, put in an appearance at the marriages, funerals, and family festivals of all classes of citizens, worked in support of some particular candidate in every election that took place, and gave hospitality in his house or provided regular assistance for a certain number of dependents among the poorer classes in Rome who served as his spies among the people, as his agents during elections, as a claque during his speeches in the Forum, or as his cutthroats in any personal quarrel.

In 68 B.C. a wonderful chance for publicity presented itself. Caesar's aunt died and Caesar was given permission to hold the usual parade and to make a speech in her honor. In these funeral processions, every patrician had the right to display the masks of his ancestors, which were usually kept in the forecourt of his house. They were worn in the parade by hired actors who represented the dead patricians. The crowds thronging the route on the day of Julia's funeral were amazed to see that among the masks of the Julians, Caesar had included that of his uncle Marius. He had neatly turned the solemn occasion into a piece of propaganda and at the same time declared that he intended to follow in the old hero's footsteps as the champion of the people's rights. The spectators roared their approval.

Roman artists in metal left an enduring record of the personalities and the daily life of their times. The statue of Caesar at right is a bronze copy, taken from the marble original, made to stand outdoors. Three coins at left show scenes of political life. At far left, on a coin minted to buy grain, two treasury officials sit between ears of wheat. On the silver penny at center is the canopied seat from which justice was dispensed, and at right a Roman citizen votes by dropping an appropriate tally into an urn.

The Romans modeled their swords on this graceful and efficient weapon, which was designed by the Spanish Celts and introduced by them into Italy during the third century B.C.

Shortly afterward, Caesar's beloved wife Cornelia also died. Caesar was once more given permission to make a speech in her honor, although this kind of tribute was not usually paid to a woman so young. Once again Caesar won the sympathy of the crowd.

In that same year, the people showed their approval in a more concrete way by electing Caesar as one of the twenty quaestors, or treasury masters. This was an important position, for upon their election, quaestors became members of the Senate. It was also the necessary first step to the office of consul.

Caesar was assigned to the province of Farther Spain, the southernmost of Rome's two Spanish provinces. His main work was the collection of duties and tributes from the scores of towns that made up the province, and in the course of these duties, he made many tours of the territory. On one of these trips to Cadiz, the Roman historian Suetonius wrote, "Caesar noticed a statue of Alexander the Great near the Temple of Hercules. Thereupon, he began to groan, and as though sickened by his inaction, thinking that he had done nothing worthy of note at an age when Alexander had already conquered the world, he immediately asked for leave of absence so that he might go to Rome and there seize the first available opportunity for distinguishing himself."

Whether this story is true or not, Caesar left Spain before the end of his year of office. There was no chance for him to make his mark as a minor official in a remote province. Rome was the political stage, and there were already many rivals contending for the limelight. Two of the leading figures in Rome at this time were Gnaeus Pompeius and Marcus Licinius Crassus.

Pompey, as he is usually called, had been one of Sulla's earliest allies. While still in his twenties he had raised and trained an army to fight for Sulla on his return from Greece. Impressed by the sight of these well-disciplined troops, Sulla had honored Pompey with the title of Imperator, or Commander, which was usually given only to generals who had won an important victory.

Acting under Sulla's orders, Pompey fought successfully against Marius' supporters in Sicily and Africa, and his reputation soared. On his return to Rome, Sulla gave him a new title, Magnus—the Great—which he added to his name and passed on to his family. In his vanity, he demanded that his several victories be celebrated with a triumphal parade. When Sulla objected, because this was not strictly legal, Pompey said insolently, "Allow me to remind you that more people worship the rising than the setting sun." He had his triumph, and all Rome turned out to cheer him.

Crassus was also an able general—he had commanded the army that finally defeated Spartacus—and a supporter of Sulla. He was one of the richest and shrewdest men in Rome. Early in his career, he had organized a fire brigade and set up lookout posts in different parts of the city. When a fire broke out, as happened all too often, the brigade rushed to the building, only to stand idle while one of Crassus' agents offered to buy it from the owner at a ridiculously low price. Only when the owner agreed to sell did the fire brigade set to work. In this way, Crassus quickly made a fortune in real estate. But neither his wealth nor his connections with Sulla nor his lavish public banquets helped to bring him the popularity that Pompey enjoyed, and he soon grew to hate Pompey.

Despite their enmity, politics brought the two men together. Both of them wanted the consulship, and they needed each other to win their goal. Pompey had never held any of the lower offices, and he needed Crassus' influence in the Senate to overcome this difficulty. Crassus hoped to share Pompey's popularity with the voters. Thus it came about that they were elected consuls for the year 70 B.C.

Caesar's reputation, while it was growing wider, was still eclipsed by these two leaders. But if he could not rival them, Caesar decided he could at least make himself useful to them. While Crassus could benefit from Caesar's con-

A picture of the Spanish tribesmen from whom Caesar collected tribute is at right—a detail from an early vase. A short warrior with a long robe and curled hair is following a taller comrade into battle.

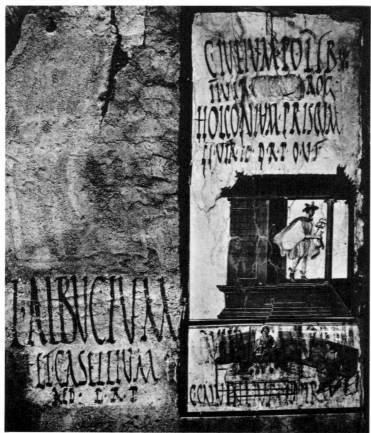

Roman election posters were written on the sides of buildings and painted over after the elections. The one above, on the wall of a clothing store, announces the candidacy of Julius Polybius and Holconius Priscus, whose names appear in the first and third lines of printing.

tacts, as he had from Pompey's, Caesar could use Crassus' wealth. Running for office was a costly business, since every candidate competed with the others in buying votes.

In 65 B.C. Caesar campaigned for the office of aedile, and Crassus supplied him with generous funds. Caesar was interested in the position because the aedile had charge of the public games and festivals. The aedileship was a first-class means of winning votes for a higher office.

Caesar was elected, and he set out to make his year of power a memorable one. During the public games in September, he gathered together so many gladiators that the Senate, fearing he was up to some mischief, set a limit on the number of men he could hire. So, instead, Caesar spent the money in equipping the men he had with silver armor. Then he persuaded his fellow aediles to spend large sums of their own money decorating the public squares and buildings, since the budget provided by the state was not enough. Caesar was always willing to spend freely, especially when the money was someone else's.

Plutarch notes that "by his great liberality and magnificence in theatrical shows, in processions, and in public feastings, he threw into the shade all the attempts that had been made before him, and . . . everyone was eager to find out new offices and new honors for him in return for his munificence."

As Caesar's popularity grew, so did the hostility of the patrician party in the Senate. They saw in him a man who would always appeal to the people in defiance of the Senate, who would try to break down their privileges, and who might even seek to become a dictator unless he was stopped. When one of the tribunes proposed that Caesar be given troops to secure Egypt and make it a Roman province, the Senate, led by the orator Cicero, refused. They would rather do without Egypt than give Caesar an army. This was a serious blow to Caesar's prestige, but undismayed, he planned a bold stroke to reinstate himself.

The High Priest of Rome had died recently, and the position was to be filled at the elections. The office of High Priest was one of the most important in the city and was usually given to a man who had seen many years of faithful service in the Senate or the army. To everyone's consternation, Caesar declared himself a candidate. He was staking his career on an enormous gamble, for his two opponents were experienced and respected men. One of them was the general to whom he had offered his services in the campaign against the pirates in 74 B.C.

Caesar planned to reduce the odds against him. He spent huge sums on his campaign, and his debts grew alarmingly. If he failed, he knew that his career would be at an end and his creditors would descend on him. But he still had a trump card to play. One of his supporters brought a law before the People's Assembly that returned to them the right to elect the High Priest. Sulla had transferred this right to the Senate, and while the Senate held it Caesar had no chance. But even when the new law was passed, Caesar felt that his prospects were doubtful. On the day of the election, he told his mother, "Today you will see your son either made High Priest or in exile."

The gamble paid off. Caesar won his election by a large majority, and he settled down in the palatial home that the state had built near the Forum for its High Priest. His position, so cleverly won, was now firmly established. Caesar had proved himself a man to watch.

The Roman priesthood held considerable political power, since every political action had to be preceded by a religious ceremony conducted by one of them. Above, a priest with a fold of his toga covering his head, offers up a sacrifice before a measure is put to popular vote.

THE TRIUMVIRATE

Caesar's enemies were alarmed by his sudden success. Despite the opposition of the patrician party, he had now reached a position of considerable power. And his election by the vote of the common people was a direct challenge to the patricians' traditional control of the government.

The rich middle class—the merchants and financiers—were equally apprehensive. Caesar, loaded down as he was with debts, had no reason to love moneylenders; nor had the common people, who were also burdened by their extortions. If Caesar chose to lead a popular revolt, the wealthy would be his first victims.

He had shown himself to be a shrewd judge of the people's moods and a master of political intrigue. He was also wise enough to keep his future plans to himself, giving his

Cicero, standing at left, hurls his denunciation from the floor of the Senate at Catiline, who sits alone, shunned by his colleagues.

45

Greatly influenced by the work of classical Greece, Roman sculptors achieved a realism unknown to the Greeks. In this portrait head of the young Caesar, the artist has not only sought to create a physical likeness but has attempted to represent the extraordinary personality of the man by modeling the work on a Greek statue of a god.

opponents no hint of what he might do next. Many of them must have recalled Sulla's words "one Caesar is worse than a dozen Mariuses," for Caesar was clearly prepared to use the mob to gain his ends if no other means presented itself. And the times were in Caesar's favor.

The period of peace that had followed the strife between Marius and Sulla was coming to an end: food shortages were common; the treasury was being drained by Pompey's recent invasion of the eastern Mediterranean; and money was scarce. Meanwhile, the struggle between the parties in the Senate was coming to a head. However, when the crisis erupted during the elections of 63 B.C., Caesar, to everyone's surprise, was not involved.

One of the candidates for the consulship was another leader of the popular party, a patrician named Catiline who had a long record of unruliness. In trying to win votes, with what he called his "clean slate," he grandly promised to cancel all debts if elected. But he made the mistake of threatening violence if he was defeated. This was nothing new for Catiline—in 66 B.C., barred from the elections because he was faced with a trial for extortion, he had plotted to murder the consuls and seize power. He had escaped punishment after the plot was uncovered only because Crassus bribed the officials who were investigating the plot.

But after Catiline lost a subsequent consular election to Cicero in 64 B.C., he received no more support from Crassus, who saw no point in backing a failure. And once again, in 63 B.C., Catiline's bid for the consulship was foiled by Cicero. During the campaign Cicero made an attack on him in the Senate, condemning him for his threats of violence, and drove the point home by appearing at the polls wearing a mail tunic under his toga and surrounded by a bodyguard of young noblemen.

Having learned nothing from his previous experience, Catiline once again hatched a plot—this time to murder Cicero and his supporters in the Senate. He began to recruit a force of gladiators and veterans from Sulla's army. When Cicero learned of the plot from one of his spies in Catiline's camp, he called on the Senate to declare martial law and bring the conspirators to justice. Catiline fled Rome, but his colleagues were arrested and thrown into prison.

In December, 63 B.C., the Senate met to discuss the fate of the prisoners. As a member of that distinguished body, Caesar was in a difficult position. The men who spoke before he did demanded the death penalty. If Caesar agreed with them, he would be condemning supporters of his own party; if he disagreed, his enemies would use it against him. When his turn came to speak, however, he was ready with a subtle argument. He pointed out that the death penalty was illegal under Roman law and that if the senators took it upon themselves to ignore the law in this case, they might just as well ignore all the laws. Many of the senators agreed with him; many more, even though they did not agree with Caesar, were unwilling to take the law into their own hands. But one young senator, an honest man and a stiff-necked conservative, was not persuaded. His name was Cato.

Cato detested everything Caesar stood for; he blamed him for all the trouble in Rome. Launching into a furious attack on Caesar, he repeated the demand for the death penalty with such force that he carried the Senate with him. The conspirators were condemned and executed. A few weeks later, Catiline led his remaining troops north in a vain attempt to escape to Gaul, but he was cut off by the Roman army and killed in the fighting.

Cato, the uncompromising foe of Caesar's ambitions, was a philosopher as well as a leader of the patricians. He committed suicide in 46 B.C., a century before this commemorative bust was sculpted.

So ended the conspiracy. It had achieved nothing except to show the corruption of Roman politics and the deep rift in the Senate. For now the party lines were clearly drawn. The patrician party, led by Cicero and Cato, both "new men," stood against the popular party led by Caesar and Crassus, both patricians by birth but popular leaders by choice. Pompey was the only important figure whose political sympathies were unknown. He had won his command in the East in 66 B.C. with the support of the popular party, but he had quarreled with Crassus, and his sympathies had always been with the patricians. Now everyone feared that when he returned to Rome, flushed with success and with an army at his back, he would follow Sulla's example and set himself up as a dictator. This was the situation when Caesar took his position as praetor, or state judge, at the beginning of 62 B.C.

He lost no time in testing his new powers. On his first day in office, he charged Catulus, the leader of the Senate, with misusing the money voted to him for repairing the Temple of Saturn. When the senators of the patrician party were told of this, they rushed to the Forum and made Caesar drop the charge. The first round had gone to his enemies, but Caesar came back to the attack by supporting a bill of one of the tribunes, Metellus Nepos, to bring Pompey back to Rome. They claimed that Pompey's troops were needed to prevent any more illegal executions. This was an attack on the senators who had condemned the conspirators, and Cato, who had also been elected a tribune, decided to use his veto against the measure. However, when he arrived in the Forum on the day the bill was to be discussed, he was attacked by a mob of Caesar's supporters and driven away battered and bleeding. He soon returned with a gang of his own men, and Caesar, in turn, was forced to beat a retreat.

After this disturbance, the Senate declared martial law and suspended Caesar from office. In protest, Caesar's supporters staged a riot outside his house and then stormed the Senate, demanding his recall. Frightened by the violence of the mob, the Senate gave way, and within a few days Caesar was back at his post.

Content with his show of strength, Caesar did nothing to trouble the peace of the city during the rest of his praetorship. However, his private life was disturbed by a scandal involving his wife, Pompeia, whom he had married shortly after Cornelia's death.

Every year a feast in honor of the *Bona Dea*—the "Good

Vain Pompey the Great (above) could never believe he needed Caesar to help him hold power.

Aristocratic matrons, like those in the Pompeian fresco at right, constituted one of the most conservative groups in Roman society. One of their duties was to conduct certain religious ceremonies, often with great mystery and secrecy.

Goddess"—was held in the house of one of Rome's leading women. No man was allowed to be present at the ceremony. In 62 B.C. Pompeia was chosen to preside over the secret rites. For some unknown reason, she smuggled into her house a disreputable young patrician named Publius Clodius disguised as a woman. Unfortunately for him, one of the matrons at the feast spoke to him, and when he replied, his voice betrayed him. The horrified woman gave the alarm, and Clodius was driven into the street.

There was an outraged uproar. Clodius was brought to trial for blasphemy, and Cicero testified against him. Yet Caesar, who was called as a witness, refused to say anything against Clodius, and Clodius himself insolently denied that he had been involved. The case was dropped, but soon afterward, Caesar puzzled everyone by divorcing Pompeia. He explained his action by saying that Caesar's family must be above even the suspicion of wrongdoing. This was taken as a joke since it was well known that Cae-

TEXT CONTINUED ON PAGE 52

TWO CENSORS were elected every five years for a term of eighteen months. They were responsible for the census of the Roman citizens, the selection of senators, and the leasing of contracts for tax collection and public building.

TWO CONSULS were elected yearly for a term of one year. They were the chief executives of the Roman government and commanders in chief of the army. They presided over the elections and the Senate, introduced laws, and held the power of veto over each other's political actions. Caesar was consul for the first time in 59 B.C.

EIGHT PRAETORS were elected yearly for a term of one year. They presided over the civil and criminal courts and deputized for the consuls when both chief executives were absent from the city. In wartime, they held high commands. Caesar was a praetor in 62 B.C.

TWENTY QUAESTORS were elected yearly for a term of one year. They were assistants to the consuls, praetors, and provincial governors, with special charge of financial matters. Two quaestors were appointed masters of the treasury in Rome, where they kept the state funds, the army standards, and the Senate records. Caesar was quaestor in Spain in 67 B.C.

PROCONSULS and PROPRAETORS governed the Roman provinces with supreme civil and military power within their territories. They were assigned their posts by the Senate, after serving a term as consul or praetor, and usually held office for one or two years. Caesar was propraetor of Spain in 61 B.C. and proconsul of Gaul 58–50 B.C.

THE SENATE consisted of six hundred members, who were selected by the censors from the patrician class and the prominent middle-class families. Consuls, praetors, quaestors, and tribunes were also members of the Senate, the tribunes only during their term of office. The Senate was the chief legislative body of the Roman state and controlled both the financial and foreign policies of the government. Its decrees became laws unless they were vetoed by the tribunes.

TEN TRIBUNES were elected yearly for a term of one year. Only plebeians could qualify for the office. The main duty of the tribunes was to safeguard the plebeians' rights by vetoing any measure of the Senate that violated them. They could also summon the People's Assembly in order to pass new laws. Caesar, being a patrician, was never a tribune.

FOUR AEDILES were elected yearly for a term of one year. They were city commissioners with many duties. They managed the markets and the public games, policed Rome, ran the fire brigade, supervised traffic, inspected weights and measures, and were generally responsible for public health and welfare. Caesar was an aedile in 64 B.C.

THE HIGH PRIEST, although he was elected, was not a political official. However, by virtue of his office, which he held for life, the High Priest had great social and political influence. Caesar became High Priest in 63 B.C.

HOW THE ROMAN GOVERNMENT WAS ELECTED

There were two voting assemblies in Rome: the Assembly of Centuries, which elected the consuls and praetors, and the Assembly of Tribes, which elected the other officials. Every citizen had the right to vote in both assemblies. In the first, the voters were divided by wealth into six classes, according to an obsolete recruiting system. Each of these classes was subdivided into a number of voting units called centuries, each of which cast one vote. Since the poorer plebeians were all grouped into one class with only five centuries, i.e. votes, they were always outvoted by the patrician and middle classes. In the Assembly of Tribes, however, every individual vote was counted, and so the plebeians held the upper hand, since they vastly outnumbered the upper classes. Yet the patricians, because they dominated the Senate and the assembly that elected the higher offices of state, still controlled the Roman government.

While entertainers like the street musicians above amused the plebeians, the patricians devoted themselves to politics. Aristocratic youths (below) formed clubs that were religious in origin and played an important part in the social and political life of the Roman state.

TEXT CONTINUED FROM PAGE 49

sar himself was no model of virtue. He had succeeded, nevertheless, in passing off what might have been a damaging incident without losing the loyalty of his followers.

In 61 B.C. Caesar was made governor of the Spanish province where he had served as a quaestor. His new responsibilities brought about a startling change in his character. He threw off his idle, pleasure-seeking way of life and proved himself an able executive and a first-class soldier.

He rejoiced in sharing the hardships of campaigning with his troops: eating the same coarse food, sleeping in the open, and marching for long hours along dusty roads and high mountain passes. He led his men in a campaign against the tribes on the Atlantic coast and added their lands to the Roman province. He also managed to settle the tangled finances of the territory. In 60 B.C. he returned to Rome, well satisfied with his work and with high hopes of being elected consul for the following year.

His victories in Spain had earned him a public triumph, and the law specified that he could not enter the city until the day of the procession. But the law also stated that he had to be in Rome on election day if he was to be a candidate. Caesar asked the Senate to allow one of his friends to represent him at the elections, but old quarrels had been neither forgiven nor forgotten. Cato persuaded the Senate to refuse. Caesar was faced with a hard choice: give up his triumph or give up his chance of election. He wisely chose to run for the consulship—triumphs could wait for another day. He was easily elected, although he was saddled with a patrician-party man, Bibulus, as co-consul.

The quarrel between Caesar and the patrician party was now clearly beyond healing, and he began to look for ways to increase his strength. He quickly found two powerful allies who had also quarreled with the Senate—his former colleagues Crassus and Pompey.

Crassus had split with the Senate when it refused to help some of his friends who had overbid for the contract to collect taxes in Asia and had failed to make any profit. They had asked the Senate to refund some of their money, but even Crassus' influence had failed to move the senators. He had taken this as a personal insult.

Pompey's quarrel was even more serious. After conquering the Eastern kingdoms, he had set them up as Roman provinces, appointing rulers who were loyal to Rome. But the Senate, determined to humiliate Pompey, had refused to approve his arrangements and had gone on to deny a grant of public land as a bonus for his troops. Pompey was infuriated.

Caesar could now deal with these two angry men on equal terms. He persuaded them to join him in a triumvirate, or three-man council, and take over the government of Rome. To cement the alliance, Caesar arranged for the

Etenim et haecuox ascendentis est pertinens ad castra ui cum gradium. deat
naq anusquisq uostrum uidere in quo profundo sit dequo clamet ad dnm
Clamauit de profundo iaçade uentre cete uel ea unon solum super fluctibus
uerameta minus certis. Belate. Nec tamen illud corpus erat ut fluctus in
terclauserunt orationem ne perueniret ad dnm et ueniet ad dm non potuit
 uel euocem ipsa uocis. penetrauit omnia dirrumpit omnia peruenit ad
aures dni. Si tamen dicendum est quia dirruptis omnibus peruenit ad aures
quando aures dni uncordi praecantis erant. ubi ei modo dirruptae sunt cum non
habet ille sed fidelis est uox. Uerumtamen et nos poti emus in illa
ce inte cum ingemiscimus inprofundo clamemus ad dnm. Profundum enim nobis est
uita ista mortalis. quisquis se in profundo intellexerit. Clamat et gea
suspirat donec de profundo eruatur. et dicet iuxta quis super omnes abis
sos se perquirit et curatus super omnia tua. cor eius non solum corpor
alia sed etiam spiritalia. Donec ad eum ueniat animo donec ad illum li ue
ueniat anima eius quae est homo. qui se illo deuin... ... tam qu
isid quis electum us ex gratia det in iesu est. et ui sibi noceat et reparet eum
ad quid illam ispraess et quando formauit hominem. Doneus esse potur bo
nus ideo casud suuar. Nor est doneus ad res tuner uone consuam. Semper
ergo quando est in isti ergo tu in dixi semper in profundo est. Sed cum
deprofundo clamat sur ei de profundo. Et ipse clamor ino deum perai
qui tu ulruin io... esse. Ualde enim in profundos sunt qui ecla
mant deprofundo. Dicit scriptura. Peccator cum uenerit in profun
dam mal orum contemnit. Jam uidete fr. quale profundum sit ubi conte
mnitur dns. Quotquot ue cider ris ex cotidianis peccatis super abun xe
uis quibusdam et uoluptatibus quibusdam iniquitatum praemittur. Si dicatur
illi ir uer tatud dm rogem in rida. quibus modis primo dicit. Si dodisph

54

Cicero (right) was a "new man," a moderate who tried to hold the middle ground between the popular and patrician extremes. He failed because he was not a practical politician. His fear of public criticism often made him irresolute; yet he had enough backbone to refuse Caesar's bribe of a partnership in the Triumvirate. Cicero's true strength lay in his unique abilities as an orator and writer. At left is a page from one of his most important works, De Republica. *The parchment on which it was written in the fourth century was scraped and reused for another work in the seventh. The Ciceronian text, in double columns, shows faintly through the later script.*

marriage of his daughter Julia to Pompey, and he himself took a third wife, Calpurnia, the daughter of one of Pompey's supporters. Then, using his power as consul, he settled his partners' grudges with the Senate. He forced the Senate to refund a third of the money that Crassus' friends had paid for the tax contract, and he brought in a bill that provided the free land for Pompey's veterans. When the Senate refused to discuss this bill, he took it to the People's Assembly. To make sure it passed, he called up Pompey's men, and when Cato tried to speak against the measure, the angry soldiers drove him from the Forum. Caesar's co-consul, Bibulus, who also tried to oppose the bill, had a basket of garbage emptied over him for his pains.

Before the Assembly Caesar revealed the existence of the Triumvirate, which until then had been a guarded secret. When the Assembly approved the land bill, Caesar turned to Pompey and Crassus, who were standing near him, and asked for their support. Pompey answered that he would defend the people's rights with sword and shield against anyone who attacked them. In one simple act, the self-appointed rulers of the Roman state showed themselves and warned their enemies that any opposition would be crushed by armed force. Having once issued this brutal threat, however, Caesar was able to introduce many valuable laws by peaceful means.

He made the Senate approve Pompey's efficient settle-

TEXT CONTINUED ON PAGE 58

The Triumvirate appears in this fifteenth-century tapestry depicting an incident in the life of Caesar. At far left, Crassus stands at his horse's

head; above him, Pompey, in an ermine-lined robe, sits in the Senate.
At right, Caesar, wearing a plumed hat, speaks to a group of kneeling Gauls.

57

One of Caesar's first tasks as proconsul was to bring his army up to strength. Thus, his officers were raising troops long before he left Rome. In the frieze at right an enlistment officer checks a recruit's name on the census roll, observed by another volunteer and an armed veteran (center). At right, Mars, god of war, stands by an altar as a sacrifice is prepared. Below is the helmet of a Gaul, soon to be a familiar sight to Caesar's troops.

TEXT CONTINUED FROM PAGE 55

ment of the new Eastern provinces and pass a second land bill that corrected some of the faults of the first. The new bill gave free land to much of Rome's overcrowded population and helped to relieve the terrible congestion in the poorer districts of the city.

He also began making plans for the following year when he would become a proconsul, or provincial governor. Before the Senate learned that the Triumvirate existed, they had appointed Caesar to the insulting post of superintendent of woods and footpaths. Now Caesar made them swallow the insult and change his appointment to the provinces of Cisalpine Gaul (the valley of the Po River) and Illyria on the east coast of the Adriatic. The thoroughly tamed Senate went even further: they added Transalpine Gaul, along the south coast of France (see map on page 124), and extended Caesar's term of office from the usual one or two years to five. No one could guess what Caesar had in mind, but no one dared to question his demands.

Once the problem of his governorship was settled, Caesar took steps to protect his position while he was away from Rome. He had his father-in-law, Piso, elected consul for the following year and made sure that his chief opponents were sent far away from Rome. Cato was given orders to dethrone the king of Cyprus and take over the island as a Roman province. Although this was an unusual and unnecessary command, Caesar knew that Cato would accept it out of a sense of responsibility. Cicero was attacked more openly. Clodius, who was now a tribune and one of Caesar's most ardent supporters, brought in a bill that outlawed anyone who had brought about the death of a Roman citizen. Cicero knew the bill was aimed at him for his part in the execution of Catiline's colleagues, and he fled Italy into self-imposed exile before he could be accused. No sooner had he left Rome than Clodius, who had held a personal grudge against him since the *Bona Dea* trial, confiscated his property and had his house burned to the ground.

At the beginning of 58 B.C., Caesar took office as governor and began to recruit troops in his provinces, although he himself seemed in no hurry to leave Rome. Then in March, news arrived that sent him hurrying north. A Germanic tribe, the Helvetii, had burned their homes and crops and were on the move. They were migrating west and threatened to cross the border of Transalpine Gaul. Caesar set out at once for his northern headquarters to take up his command. Although he could not know it, he was not to see Rome again for nine years.

This haughty warrior from a Roman legion in Spain is ready to participate in a parade. In action, his decorative but heavy crest would be discarded.

GENERAL FOR THE LEGIONS

The troops that Caesar was about to lead into Gaul were the finest in the world. They were highly trained, well-disciplined soldiers whose professionalism was actually the work of Marius. Before the time of that doughty general, fighting had been the privilege of the richer citizens who could afford their own armor and weapons. But Marius had needed more men for his wars than the rich classes could provide, and he had begun to recruit men from the landless farmers and the jobless poor who crowded the slums of Rome.

To these new soldiers the army was their career and their life. They signed on for twenty years instead of for the one or two campaigns of the old citizens' army; they fought for pay instead of glory; and they swore the oath of loyalty to their general, not to the Roman state.

Caesar's men must have waited anxiously for their new commander to arrive. Rumors of his political adventures doubtless sped on ahead of him. He had proved himself a clever vote-getter, but could he rule such a vast and rugged province as Gaul? And could he defend it?

To assist him in command, Caesar, like other Roman generals, had a staff of officers called legates. These were selected from among his friends and political allies—some because they were competent and zealous to serve Rome, others because it was expedient to give them a chance to win glory. And of course none of them were professional soldiers.

But the real backbone of the Roman army were the officers known as centurions, who trained and disciplined the troops and led them into action. The centurions' advice was so seasoned that generals often included them in war councils when planning campaigns. These proud and highly trusted officers (who would correspond to captains in a modern army) each stood at the head of a one-hundred-man unit called a century. Six such centuries made up a

SPALART, *Histoire des Costumes*, 1810

The Roman army was led into action by the standard bearers, who ranked just below the centurions. Every unit had its own standard, similar to that above, festooned with battle decorations. If a unit lost its standard, it was disgraced and sometimes even discharged.

The armor of a legionary in Caesar's army (right) was designed for efficiency, not for show. Most of it had been adapted by the Romans from the best ideas of other races. The legionary's mail tunic came originally from Gaul, the short sword from the Celts of Spain, and the helmet shape and scale armor (above) from Greece.

FERRARIO, *Il Costume Antico e Moderno*, 1815

cohort; ten cohorts, a total of six thousand fighting men, made up a full-scale Roman legion.

The men in the ranks, the foot soldiers on whom the entire army depended, were called legionaries. Their training consisted of day after day of long marches, with full equipment, inspections, and maneuvers. Special training consisted of arms drill and target practice.

The legionary's fighting equipment had been developed over centuries by trial and error. His weapons were two eight-foot javelins, which he could hurl twenty yards or more, and a short-bladed sword for hand-to-hand fighting. He carried a huge rectangular shield, which covered him from chin to ankle, and he wore a tunic of iron mail or a leather jerkin covered with overlapping iron scales. His head was protected by a helmet with a wide neckpiece and hinged iron flaps that could be swung down to cover the sides of his face.

To back up the legionaries the Roman army had a highly

Backed up by its wagon train, the massed German battle line faces a Roman army, positioned at right in the engraving above. The Romans are drawn up in their usual triple line. Carefully calculated gaps in the line allowed each battalion to maneuver independently and were covered by the units to the rear.

Construction of all kinds—forts, roads, bridges, aqueducts—marked the progress of the Roman armies. Emperor Hadrian, who completed the conquest of Britain, built this 73½-mile-long wall to protect the northern border of his new province.

advanced corps of engineers who planned and built the forts, laid out the roads, repaired the weapons, and provided the brains and muscle to man the artillery. In addition, these professional Roman fighting men were complemented by other forces recruited from the provinces and by hired mercenaries. Cavalry came from Gaul or Germany, archers from Crete and Egypt, slingers from the Balearic Islands. There was never a lack of men willing to fight for Rome in order to gain Roman citizenship.

These were the men and these the arms on which Caesar would rely. His first task was to hold back the Helvetii who were menacing his province. Some 368,000 tribesmen were gathering on the north bank of the Rhone River, which divided their land from Roman territory. Their goal was a rich portion of southwest Gaul, and their best route lay through Transalpine Gaul. And with an army of 100,000 battle-hardened warriors, they were not afraid to fight.

To stop them, Caesar had only a small part of his army —one legion and a few locally recruited troops. Undaunted by the mass of men across the river, he ordered his men to fling up fortifications along the bank and break down the only bridge, which was at Geneva. By the time the Helvetii were ready to ford the river, the Roman troops were strongly entrenched, and they hurled the tribesmen back.

While the Helvetii were looking for another way to cross the mountains that hemmed them in on all sides, Caesar sped back to Italy to bring up the rest of his army, leaving his chief of staff, Labienus, to hold the river. On his return with five fresh legions, Caesar learned that the Helvetii had discovered a pass to the north and were flooding into the territory of a Gallic tribe called the Aedui (see map on page 124), who were friends of Rome. Aeduan ambassadors arrived at his headquarters to beg for help against the invaders, and he set out at once to head them off.

Knowing that he was outnumbered three to one, Caesar was unwilling to make an open fight of it with the Helvetii. He contented himself with dogging their heels. After two weeks, however, his food began to run short. He broke off the pursuit and headed north for the Aeduan stronghold of Autun, where he could replenish his supplies.

The Helvetii mistakenly took Caesar's move for a retreat. They swung about and set off on his trail like a pack of wolves. Not far from Autun, Caesar turned at bay. With his own choice of a battleground, he hoped to counterbalance the enemy's advantage in numbers.

He drew up his troops in a triple line halfway down the slope of a steep-sided hill and posted two legions of new recruits as a reserve on the crest. When everything was ready, Caesar made a challenging speech to his men, calling upon their bravery and past victories, and then ordered all the officers' horses to be taken to the rear. There was to be no retreat from this battle.

The Helvetii reached the Roman position about midday. They wheeled into a close-packed battle line and hurled themselves on the waiting legions, hoping to overwhelm the thin lines by sheer weight of numbers. Instead they were greeted with a devastating volley of javelins that mowed down the front ranks and threw their battle line into confusion. Now generalship was called for—perfect timing above all. Before the enemy could recover, Caesar gave the order to advance, and the legions counterattacked with drawn swords.

The fury of the Roman attack drove the Helvetii off the hill and across the flat ground before it. The tribesmen were unable to make a stand until they anchored their line on another small hill about a mile from the Roman lines. Then they flung a force of fifteen thousand men onto Caesar's unprotected right flank, hoping to crush the Roman right

The ornate armor of this Roman officer is decorated with engraved and embossed designs; his golden helmet has a crest of nodding plumes. His colorful appearance allowed his soldiers to identify him easily in the confusion of the battlefield.

wing. But before this attack could be pressed home, Caesar calmly wheeled his third line to meet it, again demonstrating his natural understanding of when to play which card. And as though they were on parade, his men moved into position, continuing to advance relentlessly. Late in the afternoon the Helvetii finally broke and fled. Men, women, and children streamed northward while Caesar's cavalry hunted them down and butchered them in the thousands. A few days later, the sad, starving survivors surrendered and were ordered to return to their own lands.

No longer was Caesar a question mark to his legionaries; from the day of the victory at Autun, he was regarded as a general born to command.

As news of his victory spread through Gaul, the Gallic chieftains flocked to his headquarters to congratulate him and to assure him of their friendship. Some of them came also to beg for his help.

In one of its never-ending wars with its neighbors, a Gallic tribe called the Sequani had hired an army of German mercenaries from across the Rhine. However, when the war was over, the Germans had refused to leave. Instead, they had turned on their former employers and conquered them. The German chieftain, Ariovistus, had invited thousands of other Germans to join him, and now he was threatening to invade Gaul on a large scale.

Caesar sent a message to Ariovistus warning him that Rome would defend the rights of her allies in Gaul. The German replied insolently that Caesar had no more right in Gaul than he had and that he would smash any Roman army that dared attack him.

Caesar would not tolerate such an insult, and he marched into Sequani territory, occupying the stronghold of Besançon as a base for his attack on the Germans. The local tribesmen, who had been unable to beat the Germans, thought of them as invincible, and they began to tell the Roman troops of the incredible size and skill of the German warriors. Panic gripped Caesar's army. Men began to make their wills, officers suddenly found urgent reasons for returning to Rome, and some begged Caesar to turn back. But Caesar had an answer for them. He called a council of war and rebuked his officers for their lack of faith in him. He pointed out that the Germans were far from invincible: his uncle Marius had smashed their armies, and the recently defeated Helvetii had beaten them many times. If necessary, he said, he would march on the enemy with only his favorite legion, the Tenth.

Plunder was an important addition to the legionaries' pay, and although Caesar sought the Gauls' friendship by restraining his men, scenes such as this one from the Antonine Column in Rome were all too common. At center a barbarian mother and her son are taken prisoner, to be sold later as slaves. Above them, a bearded elder implores the gods for aid, while to the right, the Roman commander directs his men as they butcher the last few defenders.

67

His speech both shamed and inspired his men. When he led his troops out from Besançon, they were eager for battle and could not wait to come to grips with the enemy whose mere reputation had thrown them into panic only a short time before.

The two armies met about fifteen miles from the Rhine. Caesar was not as anxious as his men were for a battle; he recognized that his army was badly outnumbered. He called for a parley with Ariovistus, but their discussion solved nothing. Ariovistus remained arrogant, and his troopers broke up the meeting by attacking Caesar's bodyguard. Caesar retreated to his lines and prepared for battle.

He was puzzled by the Germans' reluctance to attack. They had the advantage of numbers, and Ariovistus had shown that he was determined to wipe out the Romans. Caesar learned the reason from some prisoners taken in a skirmish—the German priestesses had prophesied that Ariovistus would be defeated if he fought before the new moon.

The following morning, Caesar formed his troops in

John Singleton Copley, the eighteenth-century American painter, is well known for his placidly formal portraits. Yet, like many artists since Caesar's time, he was stirred by the bloody and chaotic hand-to-hand clashes of the Romans and the Gauls. He tried to catch the spirit of that violent era in his sketch, "Roman Conquest," below.

Barbarian nobles like this bearded Dacian officered the provincial troops who enlisted in the armies of Rome to earn Roman citizenship.

battle array and led them against the German camp. This was his opportunity, and he seized it eagerly. The Germans were left with no choice; the Romans were at the gates, and they had to fight despite the predictions of their priestesses. They hurled themselves on the legions with such speed that there was not time for the Romans to loose their deadly javelins. It was hand-to-hand fighting from start to finish.

Caesar led his right wing against the weaker German left, and his men cut their opponents to pieces, driving the survivors headlong from the field. However, Caesar's left flank was in trouble. Locked in the thick of the fight, he could do nothing. The day was saved by a young officer who was to serve Caesar well in the campaigns to come— Publius Crassus, the son of Caesar's colleague in the Triumvirate. Crassus called up the reserve, and the fresh troops smashed the enemy line. The Germans broke and ran for the Rhine, but few ever crossed it. Trapped on the bank by Caesar's cavalry, which had followed hot on their heels, they were hacked down without mercy. During the night Ariovistus commandeered a small boat and slipped across the river to safety, but his power was broken.

With these two campaigns, Caesar gained control of two thirds of Gaul. His speed had paralyzed the Gauls, and they did not dare to oppose him when he settled his army in their territory for the winter. He himself returned to Cisalpine Gaul to catch up with his neglected duties as governor.

All during the winter of 58–57 B.C., Caesar received a stream of disturbing reports of trouble brewing in the north of Gaul. The tribes of the Belgae, who occupied the region, were arming against a possible Roman invasion. Since any aggressive act on the part of the Belgae might lead to a rebellion among the Gallic tribes he had already subdued, Caesar decided to attack first.

As soon as the roads were passable, he led his army north in a series of forced marches. The Belgae were gathering their forces to meet him when he reached the Aisne River and crossed into their territory. Taken by surprise, they attempted to circle around his army and cut the supply lines to the south. But Caesar led a force of archers and slingers back across the river. The Belgae were ambushed and massacred as they struggled through the water. After this crushing defeat, their leaders decided that each tribe should return to its own territory and try to hold off the Romans as best it could. However, their retreat was quickly discovered by Caesar's scouts.

Caesar's army was supported by light and heavy artillery. Every century was accompanied by a dart-throwing carroballista (left)—a huge bow mounted on a horse-drawn carriage and operated by a crew of five engineers. Larger types of catapults, which fired javelins or heavy rocks, were used at sieges and to defend the legionary camps.

Caesar could not believe their reports; he was convinced the Belgae were trying to lead him into a trap. After two days of indecision, during which the Belgae continued to make for their homes, Caesar realized that they really were retreating, and he let loose his cavalry to hunt them down. The orderly Belgian withdrawal was turned into a bloody rout.

The resistance of the Belgae was finished. Tribe after tribe surrendered as the legions marched down the Aisne River, storming stronghold after stronghold. At last only a small group of tribes in the far north was left. Their leaders were the Nervii, the most warlike of the Belgae, and they had sworn to defy the Romans to the last man. Caesar was determined to leave no spark of resistance burning, and he marched north to the Sambre River, where the Nervii were preparing their last-ditch stand.

The Roman troops reached the riverbank in the late afternoon and began to build their camp. Suddenly the Nervii poured out of the wooded hills on the opposite bank and swept down on the straggling legions. For the first— and only—time, Caesar had been taken by surprise. His men did not even have time to put on their helmets or join their own units; they formed lines wherever they could. The cavalry and the archers, scattered by the first charge, fled to the rear, leaving the legionaries to face the enemy alone.

In the early days of the republic, cavalry was provided by the wealthy class of Romans; but as the empire expanded, and with it the army, mounted troops were recruited in the provinces. The horsemen from a Roman carving at right may be Gauls, who were renowned for their equestrian skill and provided much of the Roman auxiliary cavalry.

Caesar was everywhere at once, pushing his men into line, shouting encouragement, trying to prevent them from huddling together. On the left flank the Twelfth Legion had been hardest hit; most of the centurions were dead or wounded, and their legionary standard had been captured. When Caesar arrived, he found the men tired and ready to surrender. Taking a shield from one of the soldiers in the rear rank, he rode out in front of the legionaries and ordered them to follow him. At once the men's spirits rose, and they began to fight with renewed courage.

Even so, the situation was desperate. The fury of the Nervii warriors was beginning to wear down the legionaries. Then, at the blackest moment, Labienus appeared on the crest of the hills across the river with the two legions that had formed the rear guard. He sent them charging down on the enemy's rear. There could be only one end to the battle now. The Nervii were outnumbered, and surrounded by fresh troops, but they fought on with remarkable courage. As their front ranks fell, the men behind scrambled onto the wall of bodies and continued to fight, catching Roman javelins as they flew and hurling them back. As night fell on the scene of carnage, the Nervii had almost fulfilled their oath. Of the sixty thousand men who had charged down the hill at the beginning of the battle, only five hundred were left.

Caesar was careful to protect the survivors among the Nervii, now mostly old men, women, and children. He admired the courage of their fighting men and took no steps against them. They were allowed to return to their homes, and Caesar warned their enemies to leave them in peace.

Only one tribe, the Atuatuci, were still holding out. They had taken refuge in their strongest fortress when they heard that Caesar had defeated the Nervii and was advancing north against them. Caesar was prepared for a long siege, but the speed with which his engineers flung up their fortifications and built their siege towers frightened the Atuatuci into surrender—or so it appeared. Under cover of night, however, the tribesmen broke out and made a treacherous assault on the Roman lines. They thought they would catch the legions off guard, but they were sadly mistaken. Caesar had ordered his sentries to be especially alert, and the alarm was given. The Atuatuci were driven back into the town with heavy losses, and the following day the Romans occupied the fortress. As an example to all who dared to rebel against the might of Rome, Caesar sold the entire population into slavery. He admired courage but gave short shrift to treachery.

Gaul now seemed to be cowed by Caesar's power, and he decided that it was safe to return to his province. Despite the long, hard campaign of the previous summer, he tackled his responsibilities with unfailing energy—administering justice, gathering fresh supplies for the army, recruiting replacements for his legions, and catching up with the latest news from Rome.

The Senate had decreed a public thanksgiving of fifteen days to honor Caesar's victories in Gaul. The Romans felt that a new province had been secured, although Caesar still had his doubts. Even so, he was pleased by the honor, for it was the longest thanksgiving that had ever been held. But otherwise the news from Rome was bad. Cato was due to return from Cyprus and could be counted on to mount a fresh attack on Caesar. Meanwhile, Pompey and Crassus were at each other's throats once again, and there was grave danger that the Triumvirate would fall apart.

Caesar summoned his colleagues to a meeting at Luca, in the north of Italy, and presented a new scheme to them. Pompey and Crassus were to become consuls for the year

In a relief from the Roman triumphal arch at Carpentras, France, two captive Gauls stand miserably chained to a trophy of their surrendered arms.

56 B.C. and would arrange for Caesar's command to be extended for another five years. Then when Caesar returned to Rome, he would become consul, while his partners would be appointed to important governorships. In this way the Triumvirate would retain control of the government and would have an army at its command at all times. For the moment Pompey and Crassus agreed to follow this plan. They made peace, and the three partners renewed their promises of mutual support.

Satisfied that his most pressing problems at home had been settled, Caesar set out for his Illyrian province in the early spring. Then an urgent message arrived from young Crassus. The Veneti, a seafaring people who lived on the south coast of the Cherbourg peninsula, were stirring up trouble on Gaul's Atlantic coast. They had captured the Roman quartermasters who were seeking supplies for the legions and were now urging their neighbors to revolt.

Caesar turned back to Gaul at once. He scattered his troops throughout Gaul to prevent the rebellion from spreading. Then he flung a cordon of troops around the territory of the Veneti to isolate them and ordered a fleet to be built on the Loire River—a seafaring people would have to be beaten on sea as well as on land. While his orders were being carried out he led a striking force into the Cherbourg peninsula.

The campaign was nothing but frustration for Caesar. The towns of the Veneti were built at the ends of narrow capes and headlands along the coast. As soon as the Romans appeared, the inhabitants simply boarded their ships, and contemptuous of the land-bound Romans, sailed off to the next town to take up the battle again.

At last the Roman fleet was ready, and it set off for the Cherbourg peninsula to link up with Caesar. The opposing navy—a Gallic armada of over two hundred ships—sailed out to meet it. The vessels of the Veneti had a great advantage: they were oaken sailing ships, and their high sides allowed the crews to fire missiles down on the Roman galleys, which sat low in the water. The Roman ships, built in the traditional Mediterranean way, were driven by oars and equipped with rams, which were useless against the stout sides of the Venetian vessels. However, Roman ingenuity overcame the disadvantage. Caesar's men were supplied with long hooked poles with which they tore down the enemy's rigging. The Veneti were helpless once their sails had collapsed. Even the weather turned against them: the wind died away before any of their ships could escape

This fifteenth-century tapestry depicting Caesar's life shows Ariovistus (mounted at top right) as a knight charging into the conflict.

In 107 B.C. the Helvetii crushed a Roman army barring their invasion of Transalpine Gaul. In this painting by the Swiss artist Charles Gleyres, the Roman survivors pass under the yoke— the most degrading form of surrender—between the impaled heads of their generals. The Romans' shame at this defeat was finally erased by Caesar's victory over the Helvetian forces at Autun.

to the open sea. The Roman galleys ran alongside, and the troops swarmed aboard. They hurled the Veneti into the sea or cut them down as they fought on decks slippery with blood. By sunset the Roman victory was complete. A few battered remnants of the once-proud Venetian fleet slipped away in the dusk and made for the shore, where their crews spread the tragic news to their fellow tribesmen.

All Gaul had been pacified—for the moment. However, at the beginning of 55 B.C., a new threat appeared from a different quarter. Two German tribes crossed the Rhine and invaded the territory of the Belgae. They spread across the land, looting and burning, while refugees streamed south to carry word of the German horde.

In the spring Caesar called up the legions that had been stationed in Normandy during the winter to cut off

The Veneti were defeated by ships similar to this Roman war galley. They were driven by two banks of oars and carried crews of marines who boarded the enemy as archers fired missiles from their towers.

the German advance. At once their chieftains begged for a parley. They explained that they were not in Gaul by choice but because they had been driven from their own homes by the mighty Suebi, another German people who lived to the east of them. They asked Caesar's permission to settle in the Belgian land they had taken, but he refused to discuss the matter until they had returned back across the Rhine. The chieftains asked for time to consider their plans, and Caesar agreed to this. When they asked for more time, however, Caesar began to suspect they were plotting some kind of treachery. Then his scouts reported that German troops were scattered around the countryside looking for plunder, and he finally realized that the Germans were merely playing for time while they gathered their army together.

When a third delegation arrived at Caesar's camp to ask for still more time, he had them arrested, and then marched on their camp with his usual speed. Taken by surprise, the Germans fled before the attack. Caesar sent his cavalry to hunt them down, and a terrible slaughter ensued in which men, women, and children alike were butchered.

Caesar's enemies in Rome used reports of the massacre as an excuse to attack him politically; Cato even suggested that Caesar's conduct had been so brutal that he himself should be handed over to the Germans. But Caesar was determined to teach the Germans a lesson they would never forget. He ordered his engineers to build a bridge across the Rhine, and although the river was wide and the current swift, his men constructed a bridge forty feet wide in only ten days. Caesar led his troops into Germany, and for eighteen days, devastated the countryside. Then, on hearing that a vast German army was gathering against him, he marched back into Gaul, smashing the bridge behind him.

Caesar's thoughts were now turning in a new direction —toward Britain. This island had become a refuge for rebel Gauls who escaped from Caesar's clutches, and the Britons had encouraged the Gauls in their revolts. Besides, Caesar was curious to see this land about which the Romans knew so little. He ordered the fleet to sail up the coast and meet him at Boulogne. Fully confident in his generalship, he embarked two legions and some cavalry and set sail for Britain, even though the season was late and the enemy unknown.

To prevent Caesar's Rhine bridge from being carried away, his engineers anchored the upstream piers (at right in this model) to massive stakes and braced the downstream piers with heavy angled buttresses.

77

"All Gaul is divided into three parts" are the famous opening words of Caesar's Commentaries. *The three parts are shown clearly in this map from a 1513 edition of his great work. In the north lived the Belgae, who were of Germanic origin; in the southwest, the Aquitani; the rest of Gaul, as well as Britain, was occupied by Celts. Caesar was an accurate observer, and his description of the Gauls is a major source of material for scholars.*

V

CAMPAIGN OF CONQUEST

The August sunlight glinted on the oar blades of the massed Roman fleet as it surged toward the shores of Britain. At Caesar's command, the war galleys swept ahead to run up on the beach while their crews fired a hail of missiles into the British battle line at the water's edge. The deeper Roman troopships grounded in the shallows, and the order was passed for the legionaries to attack. For minutes not a man moved. Faced with a struggle through the water at the mercy of a well-prepared foe, Caesar's men faltered. Then the standard-bearer of the Tenth Legion flung himself into the sea, calling for his comrades to follow. Inspired by his courage, they poured from the ships and staggered after him.

The fight to win the rocky beach was bitter and confused as Britons and Romans struggled in the bloodstained surf. But British speed and daring were no match for Roman discipline. As soon as the legions formed their well-ordered lines and charged, the Britons were swept away in wild disorder. However, there was no cavalry to complete the legionaries' work. Their transports had gone astray during the crossing, and for the moment, Caesar had to be content with half a victory.

Similar frustrations dogged all his efforts at conquest. After the bloody lesson on the beach, the Britons refused to fight in the open. Instead, they waged a deadly guerrilla war from the cover of their dense forests. Swift British chariots struck again and again at the slow-moving Roman columns moving inland; stragglers were ambushed, and foraging parties, searching for food and fuel, were surrounded and butchered.

Caesar soon found that he could not beat the Britons at this kind of fighting, and to add to his troubles, his fleet anchored in the Channel was being battered by autumn storms. As summer came to an end, he beat a retreat to Gaul, empty-handed and angry.

He ordered an armada to be built, and all during the

The emblem of the Twentieth Legion, a wild boar, is displayed on this roof tile from Chester, England. "Chester" derives from the Latin word castra, *an army camp.*

winter months an army of Roman engineers and Gallic craftsmen slaved to complete the project. By spring of 54 B.C., eight hundred ships were ready to sail. Before Caesar left, however, he took hostages from all the Gallic tribes to ensure peace while he was away. One of them, the Aeduan nobleman Dumnorix, outraged at this treatment, resisted and tried to escape. Caesar was forced to execute him as a warning to the others, although he knew this would offend many of his Gallic allies. Still, by midsummer, Caesar judged that it was safe to return to Britain. He ferried five legions and four thousand cavalry across the Channel, intent on wiping out his previous failure.

Caesar was also spurred on to invade Britain a second time by a new spirit of imperial conquest that had recently seized and excited the Roman ruling classes. Sturdy Celtic slaves to be sold in Mediterranean markets were as much desired as ever; tin and other useful metals continued to be needed from British mines. But even more important than these was the prospect of planting the standards of Rome in the very corners of the known world.

At first it appeared that Caesar would indeed be able

In the manuscript illumination below, Caesar (bare-headed at far left) orders his men ashore on the British coast. The artist, in the convention of his time, shows the Romans as fourteenth-century knights and the Britons as bowmen. In fact, the invaders were met by war chariots (above).

to carry out that proud purpose. His landing on the southeast coast of Britain was not opposed, and on the following day he routed the native forces in a major battle near present-day Canterbury. The Britons, regrouping in retreat, were able for the first time to achieve a measure of unity under a king named Cassivellaunus. Retreating to the north bank of the Thames River, their hope was to lure Caesar away from his coastal supply camp and into a trap among the unfamiliar bogs and forests of the interior. Meanwhile they plagued his army with hit-and-run raids and sudden ambushes. And once again, gales wrecked the Roman troopships lying at anchor and flooded the war galleys drawn up on the shore.

Since armed strength would not serve to clinch the expected conquest of Britain, Caesar turned to intrigue. He made an alliance with a British king who had sought him out in Gaul the year before. Soon, other tribal leaders, more fearful of the Roman army than of the wrath of their fellow Britons, followed suit. By these tactics, he was able in a few weeks to crush the British forces that were still holding out and to patch up a kind of peace that for the time being would have to take the place of an imperial conquest. For news had reached Caesar that the Gauls were again rising against Rome, despite the fact that Caesar was holding their leaders as hostages. So, although he knew that his hold on Britain was far from secure, as autumn approached, Caesar reluctantly set sail from that island, never to return.

Caesar had always feared a general uprising in Gaul, and he felt that he had never had enough troops to hold all the vast territory he had conquered. His whirlwind campaigns had left the Gauls dazed rather than defeated, and now the shock was beginning to fade. The execution of Dumnorix had angered the Gauls, as Caesar feared it would, and a poor harvest after a long drought added fuel to the flames. The Roman quartermasters took most of the crops for the legions, leaving little for the Gauls. In the end, hunger drove them to open rebellion.

Because of the food shortage, Caesar had been forced to establish his winter camps far from one another. This scattered line of defense was too great a temptation for a Belgian chieftain named Ambiorix. He flung a cordon of men around a camp commanded by the two legates Sabinus and Cotta. He asked for a parley with them, and pretending friendship, told them that all the Gallic tribes, supported by Germans, were up in arms. He offered the garrison a safe-conduct as far as the nearest Roman camp, claiming that he did so out of gratitude for Caesar's many kindnesses. Cotta suspected a trap, but he was overruled by Sabinus, who was made anxious by Ambiorix' lying tale. And so the next morning the Roman troops marched out with their baggage train.

At first it seemed as though Ambiorix meant to keep his word—not a Gaul was in sight. But the Belgian chief was merely biding his time. As the Roman column entered a wooded ravine two miles from the camp, his warriors sprang from their ambush among the trees and blocked the road. A deadly rain of missiles poured down on the Roman soldiers huddled below. Sabinus, realizing too late that he had been tricked, tried to find Ambiorix to plead for a truce, only to be surrounded and killed. Cotta, although badly wounded in the face, formed his men into a circle and fought grimly on. Outnumbered, outmaneuvered, and faced with certain death, the Romans sold their lives gallantly. One centurion continued to lead his men, though both his thighs had been pierced by javelins; another centurion fell while struggling to rescue his own son who had been surrounded by the enemy.

Despite their desperate defense, the Romans were overwhelmed at last by a massive Gallic charge. Cotta died fighting in the ranks as a few stragglers who had escaped the carnage slipped away through the forest to carry news of the disaster to Caesar.

Ambiorix, elated by his success, carried the message of revolt through all the northern tribes. Among the first to join him were the Nervii, still smarting from their defeat at Caesar's hands. Their leaders decided to try Ambiorix'

TEXT CONTINUED ON PAGE 86

Cotta has marshaled his troops into a defensive circle in this illustration from an eighteenth-century edition of Caesar's Commentaries. *The figure on horseback in the center of the ring (letter B) is the Roman general directing the defense. In front of him, at right, a section has left its post in a useless attempt to break through the Gallic army surrounding them.*

83

The Romans had little idea of the geography of their world. This map of Europe, an exact thirteenth-century copy from the Roman original of the third century A.D., makes no attempt to show the size, the shape, or even the true position of the various geographical features. Rivers all run from east to west, even the Rhine (at extreme top), which actually

flows from south to north. Paris ("Parisi" in upper right corner) is north of Belgium ("Belgi" in red letters), and the Italian peninsula does not appear at all in the wide olive-brown stripe of the Mediterranean. However, in one way the map is amazingly precise—distances between towns are shown accurately, indicating that it was a road map.

TEXT CONTINUED FROM PAGE 82

ruse on Quintus Cicero, the orator's younger brother, who commanded the Roman troops stationed in their territory. But Cicero was not fooled by their lies. He ordered his men to secure the camp and prepare for battle.

The Nervii settled down to besiege him. They had learned something of siege warfare from watching the Romans, and they had Roman prisoners to direct their efforts. In a short time they had encircled the camp with a huge rampart, the dirt for which had been dug up with sword blades and even bare hands and carried in their cloaks.

Cicero tried desperately to get word to Caesar, but his messengers were captured and then tortured in full view of the camp. At last one broke through. He was the personal slave of a friendly Belgian nobleman in the camp, and being a Gaul himself, he was able to slip unchallenged through the Nervian lines with the message wound around the shaft of his spear.

As he sped toward Caesar's headquarters, a savage battle broke out around the camp. Attack after attack was hurled back by the Roman garrison until the ground before the walls of the camp was heaped with Gallic corpses. Then the Nervii set fire to the wooden huts inside the compound, and before long the whole camp was ablaze. The legionaries held their posts and continued to fight amid the roaring flames and swirling black smoke.

Then one morning a sentry on the wall noticed a spear lodged in one of the towers. Fastened to the shaft was a message written in Greek so that the Gauls would not be able to read it if it fell into their hands. It was Caesar's reply, flung into the camp by his messenger two days before, and unseen in the chaos of battle. Caesar was on his way to the rescue with two legions. The news brought fresh hope to Cicero's weary, wounded men, and they returned to the fight with renewed vigor.

The next day the distant smoke of burning Gallic villages warned the Nervii of Caesar's approach, and they abandoned the siege to turn about and face him. Caesar was warned of the move by a dispatch from Cicero, and he entrenched his troops behind a stream. The following morning, the Nervii, sixty thousand strong, launched a confident attack on Caesar's small force. But although they outnumbered the Romans nearly ten to one, they overrated

The Gauls were an agricultural people (right) who lived in tribal communities ruled by councils of noblemen like the one above in hunting costume.

The territory of the Belgae and the Germans is shown in the seventeenth-century map above. Three quarters of it is covered with dense woods, where the Germans took refuge during Caesar's raids. The Ardennes Forest ("Arduenna"), home of Ambiorix and the Nervii, is above the panel in the lower left corner. Typical of their fighting men are the four warriors at right; a trumpeter, a cavalryman, a standard-bearer, and a chief in winged helmet.

themselves. A single disciplined charge by the legions scattered them like chaff. Throwing down their weapons in panic, they fled for the woods, where the hotly pursuing Roman troops butchered them by the score.

For the remainder of the winter, an uneasy peace descended on Gaul, but Caesar had new woes to face. In the fall, his beloved daughter Julia had died. Caesar's grief was intensified by the knowledge that his most important tie with Pompey was gone and his carefully constructed triumvirate was in danger. For some time Pompey had been drifting back to the patrician side, where his true sympathies lay. Crassus might have held him to his allegiance, but their old quarrels had flared up again. Besides, Crassus was more interested in readying an expedition against the Parthians, whose rich empire sprawled to the east of Asia Minor. Still envious of his colleague's military renown, he was prepared to sacrifice the Triumvirate to his personal ambition. Caesar, forced to remain far from Rome, was helpless.

His own reputation had been tarnished too, not only by the fiasco in Britain but by the conduct of his supporters in Rome. Clodius had been elected tribune with Caesar's support, but power had gone to his head. He raised gangs

TEXT CONTINUED ON PAGE 92

FIGHTING MEN OF GAUL

By Caesar's time, the Gauls were a settled, productive people, quite different from their warlike ancestors who had raided into Italy and sacked Rome itself in the fourth century B.C. Yet, even though the Gauls had lost some of the spirit of their forefathers, they were still formidable opponents. The bulk of their armies was an infantry force of peasants, untrained but seasoned by the constant fighting among the tribes. However, their real strength lay in their magnificent cavalry, drawn from the ruling class of noblemen. The aristocratic warrior at left, his rank proclaimed by the torque, or gold collar, around his neck, was well equipped for war. His armor consisted of a mail shirt, a large shield, and a helmet (below, left) richly embossed and crusted with gems. His favorite weapon was a long, double-edged slashing sword (far left). Led into battle behind standards bearing the figure of a wild boar, symbol of their war-god (below, right), these hardy warriors defended their land for nine years against the armed might of Rome and the military genius of their final conqueror, Julius Caesar.

TEXT CONTINUED FROM PAGE 89

of ruffians to bully his political enemies, and he terrorized Rome into submission. His men beat and robbed passers-by and looted houses with impunity. Another tribune, Milo, raised similar gangs to oppose Clodius, but instead of restoring peace, the rival gangs turned the streets of Rome into shambles. The patrician party, which secretly backed Milo, blamed the bloodshed on Caesar. But at that moment Caesar's mind was taken up with more urgent matters.

The slippery Ambiorix had escaped unhurt from the battle at Cicero's camp and was once more preaching rebellion in northern Gaul. Caesar sent out three flying columns to hunt him down, but without success. Although the Romans marched back and forth, stamping out the revolts that sprang up in Ambiorix' wake, they could not corner him. At last Caesar called off the chase and ordered his men to put the countryside to the torch. Crops and houses were burned, and cattle were driven off to swell the Roman supplies. Then while his army settled into winter quarters, Caesar returned to Cisalpine Gaul.

News of fresh disasters awaited him there. Crassus and his army had been massacred by the Parthians at Carrhae, and Clodius too had been killed. He had run into one of Milo's gangs and had been murdered in the streets. Caesar, however, had no time to counteract these setbacks. The Gauls were planning another rising, and this time they had a leader whom all the tribes of Gaul were willing to follow —a young nobleman called Vercingetorix.

Vercingetorix was a remarkable man. By sheer strength of will, he welded the mass of warring tribes into a single force and held it together by savage discipline. With a vast army at his back, he was planning to invade the Roman province of Transalpine Gaul—and perhaps Italy itself.

Caesar realized that the final struggle for supremacy in Gaul was at hand. Hurriedly he organized the defenses of Narbonne, the chief city of Transalpine Gaul, and then set out to join his legions in northern Gaul.

The rebel forces held central Gaul, blocking his path. Only the rugged Cévennes mountain range to the north of

TEXT CONTINUED ON PAGE 96

The gigantic ramp that enabled Caesar's troops to storm Bourges is hidden between the two towers in the center of the model at right above. The siege works at Alesia (right, below) were even more extensive. In front of the moated wall is a fence of tangled branches and a checkerboard of circular pits with sharpened stakes that the Roman troops called "lilies." In front of these are the "goads," barbed iron hooks sunk into buried logs.

GABINETTO FOTOGRAFICO NAZIONALE, ROME

MUSÉE DES ANTIQUITÉS NATIONALES, ST. GERMAIN EN LAYE: GIRAUDON

THE SIEGE OF ALESIA

Alesia stood on an unassailable, steep-sided hill. It was held by Vercingetorix' army of 80,000 men, along with an adjoining camp on the eastern slope. Since an assault was impossible, Caesar decided to trap the garrison and starve it out. The town was encircled by a turf wall, twelve feet high and nine miles long, surmounted with a breastwork of woven branches and towers for catapults and archers. Two ditches, the inner one filled with water, were dug at the base of the wall, and the ground before it was sewn with booby traps— first, a line of pits filled in with tangled boughs, known as "tombstones" to Caesar's soldiers; then, rows of "lilies," which were covered with brushwood to conceal them; and finally, the barbed "goads" to catch the feet of the defenders. Two wide ditches were also dug at the bottom of the hill, from east to west, to break up the defenders' sorties. The besiegers lived in eight camps and twenty-three forts scattered along the wall. A second similar fortification, thirteen miles long, was built around the first to protect it from assault by a relieving army of Gauls who had arrived to rescue Vercingetorix. The view of the siegeworks above—the most elaborate ever undertaken by Caesar's engineers —is from the Gauls' camp on the neighboring heights.

Eius adventu ex colore vestitus cognito, quo insigni in proeliis uti consuerat, turmisque equitum et cohortibus visis quas se sequi iusserat, ut de locis superioribus haec declivia et devexa cernebantur, hostes proelium committunt. Utrimque clamore sublato excipit rursus ex vallo atque omnibus minitionibus clamor. Nostri emissis pilis gladiis rem gerunt. Repente post tergum equitatus cernitur; cohortes aliae appropinquant. Hostes terga vertunt; fugientibus equites occurrunt. Fit magna caedes. Sedulius dux et princeps Lemovicum acciditur; Vercassinellaunus Arvernus vivus in fuga comprehenditur: signa militaria septuaginta quattuor ad Caesarem referuntur: pauci ex tanto numero se incolumes in castra recipiunt. Conspicati ex oppido caedem et fugam suorum desperata salute copias a munitionibus reducunt. Fit protinus hac re audita ex castris Gallorum fuga. Quod nisi crebris subsidiis ac totius diei labore milites essent defessi, omnes hostium copiae deleri potuissent. De media nocte missus equitatus novissimum agmen consequitur: magnus numerus capitur atque interficitur; reliqui ex fuga in civitates dicedunt. DE BELLO GALLICO, LIBER VII, 88.

This is a passage from Caesar's De Bello Gallico, *his own account of the conquest of Gaul. He completed the seven books of commentaries in under two months while wintering near Autun in 52–51 B.C. Despite this, his work is considered among the finest in classical literature and has been used as a model of prose style for centuries.*

TEXT CONTINUED FROM PAGE 92

Transalpine Gaul had been left unguarded, for the Gauls thought the snow-choked passes were unusable at that time of year. However, Caesar led a small force of cavalry through the six-foot drifts, and while his men made a feint to draw off Vercingetorix' troops, Caesar, alone and unguarded, slipped north along the Saône River to his headquarters.

Once more in command of the situation, Caesar gathered his scattered garrisons together and launched a major offensive against Vercingetorix. He sent Labienus to pacify the northern tribes while he himself marched west, storming one rebel stronghold after another across central Gaul. Then he turned south to begin an assault on Vercingetorix' own territory. The Gallic chief retreated before the invaders and fell back. His warriors burned their villages and destroyed their crops to keep anything of value from falling into Roman hands. Only the town of Bourges held out; it was well fortified and stood amid marshes and streams that made a strong natural defense. Caesar's engineers quickly threw up siegeworks around the town and began to build an enormous ramp over three hundred feet

CAESAR'S *War Commentaries*. ED. & TRANS. BY JOHN WARRINGTON. DUTTON EVERYMAN PAPERBACK, 1958

The enemy recognized my scarlet cloak, and then saw my combined force moving down the slopes, which were clearly visible from Mont Rea. As they enjoined battle both sides raised a cheer which was taken up by the soldiers on the rampart and along the whole line of fortifications. The legionaries dispensed with pikes and had got to work with their swords when the Gauls suddenly beheld our mounted squadrons in their rear as fresh battalions of infantry closed in from the south. They broke and fled, but were intercepted by the cavalry and mown down. Sedulius, chief magistrate and commander of the Lemovices was killed; Vercassivellaunus was taken prisoner in the rout; and I was presented with seventy-four Gallic standards. Very few of that great army got back safely to camp. Vercingetorix witnessed the rout and slaughter of his countrymen: he gave up all hope, and withdrew once again into Alesia, while the camp on Mussy-la-Foss was hurriedly abandoned. Were it not for the fact that our men were tired out after a long day's work, in the line or in reserve, the entire enemy force might well have been annihilated. As it was, the cavalry went out just after midnight and overtook their rearguard, many of whom were cut down or taken prisoner. The survivors made for home.

long and seventy feet high. Many of the Gauls inside the town were skilled miners, and they tunneled beneath the ramp and set it on fire. At the same time, the gates of Bourges opened and a party of Gauls rushed out to feed the flames with pitch and tallow. One after another they were shot down by Roman catapult fire, but as each man fell another took his place. They held their perilous position by the ramp until the Romans finally doused the fire.

The following day, in a heavy rain, the ramp was finally finished. The Gallic sentries did not think the Romans would attack in such bad weather, and they were taken by surprise when Caesar's men charged up the ramp and over the walls of Bourges. Within minutes they had taken the walls and were pouring into the narrow streets of the town, smashing the last stand of the garrison in the market square and cutting down the townspeople as they crowded in panic through the narrow gateways. Only a handful survived to carry the news to Vercingetorix. But defeat could not shake the Gauls' confidence in their young leader; even the Aedui, Caesar's oldest allies in Gaul, went over to the rebel's side. And Vercingetorix' popularity soared to new heights when a few weeks later he forced the Roman army to withdraw from his own city of Gergovia.

Then, through overconfidence, he blundered. He ordered his cavalry to attack Caesar's army as it moved toward its base in Aeduan country. Caesar had been reinforced by a strong force of horsemen recruited among friendly German tribes. Backed up by the legions, who were far from dispirited, the Germans hurled back the Gallic assault. As the survivors fled before the victorious Germans, the Gallic infantry stationed nearby panicked and fled. They did not stop running until they reached the fortress of Alesia a short distance away.

The following day, Caesar surrounded the town, which stood on a high hill. He set his engineers to work encircling the fortress with a wall in order to cut Vercingetorix off from outside help. Nine miles of fortifications were laid out, and the labor began while the German cavalry held off Gallic raids. Before the wall was completed, a few of Vercingetorix' cavalry escaped and set off to bring aid to the beleaguered garrison. Soon, a Gallic army of more than a quarter-million men was on its way to rescue its leader.

When Caesar learned of this, he built a second ring of defenses thirteen miles long to face this new threat. He knew that Vercingetorix was in desperate need of food. Even though all civilians had been driven out of Alesia, supplies were running short. In desperation Vercingetorix hurled his troops at the Roman walls day and night. But each time, Caesar's men rose to the challenge and drove them back into the town. At last the Gauls decided to stake everything on one massive assault: while the forces outside attempted to breach Caesar's fortifications at the western end, the defenders of Alesia would attack from within.

When the signal was given, wave after wave of Gauls smashed against the Roman defenses. All along the walls there was furious fighting. But Caesar and his lieutenants were everywhere, rallying their men and bringing up reinforcements to fling the attackers back. As the sun began to drop toward the hills, the fury of the assault died away. Caesar, his scarlet cloak flying in the wind, rallied his tired men and led a counterattack while his cavalry swept around the rear of the enemy outside. The Gauls broke and ran into the gathering dusk. Vercingetorix, seeing the end of his hopes, led his forces back into Alesia for the last time. The next morning he rode down to the Roman walls to lay his weapons at Caesar's feet in token of surrender.

A dead Gallic soldier from Alesia wears the typical costume of his people—long breeches, belted at the waist, and heavy leather boots.

The defeat of Vercingetorix was not the end of the fighting in Gaul. Caesar still faced another year of battles before he could claim that Gaul was truly a part of the Roman Empire. But after Alesia, the Gallic resistance lost strength, and without Vercingetorix, the Gauls were disorganized and broken.

By the end of 51 B.C. Caesar's conquest of Gaul was complete, and his troops were stationed in well-positioned fortresses across the land. With ten years of command coming to an end, Caesar could look back with satisfaction on his campaigns, but he could also look forward to battles with another, older foe—the patrician party. For Caesar was about to embark on the last and most important campaign of his career.

A long-haired warrior slashes in vain at a plundering legionary in a scene that must have been repeated often during the conquest of Gaul. In the background is the warrior's wooden hut with its thatched roof.

VI ACROSS THE RUBICON

In this Renaissance tapestry, Caesar, on the white horse at left, prepares
to cross the Rubicon, the first of many obstacles on his road to supremacy.

With his provincial command in Gaul scheduled to end, Caesar had to consider his future in Roman politics. His chief object was to become consul for the year 48 B.C. Election for the office would be held in the middle of 49 B.C., and Caesar wanted to make sure there would be no barriers to block him.

He knew that senatorial opposition to him was intense. His political beliefs, together with his military renown and his popularity with the masses, made many senators wary of his election to the consulship. The patricians feared that the constitutional government of the republic would

The Roman author Lucan wrote that on the night before Caesar crossed the Rubicon, he dreamed that the spirit of Rome begged his army to halt on the riverbank. Suetonius added that an unearthly being who had been sitting playing a reed pipe as Caesar approached snatched a trumpet from one of the soldiers, blew a loud blast, and crossed the stream. Caesar ordered his army to follow, crying, "The die is cast." The medieval illustrations of this incident above and at right combine elements from both accounts.

102

be destroyed if he became consul. Cato even wanted to have Caesar punished for alleged misdeeds by exiling him once his command in Gaul ended.

Caesar hoped to circumvent this hostility by taking advantage of a law that had been passed for his special benefit three years before. This law conferred upon a governor the privilege of standing for the consulship *in absentia*. Caesar also hoped to receive an extension of his provincial command until he was actually elected consul. If both these hopes were realized, he would not have to return to Rome as a private citizen, and, as consul-elect, he would be safe from any attack.

The Senate, however, was determined to take every measure to block Caesar. It refused to prolong his command and decided to discuss the question of his successor in Gaul at the earliest opportunity. This presented an immediate danger; since he was so far removed from Rome, Caesar had to find a way to protect his interests.

He enlisted the aid of a young and skillful tribune

Mark Antony was one of Caesar's strongest allies, even though his grandfather had been executed by Caesar's uncle, Marius. Antony was described by the historian Plutarch as having ". . . a very good and noble appearance . . . a bold, masculine look that reminded people of the appearance of Hercules in paintings and sculptures."

named Curio by promising to pay off his debts and to reward him liberally with additional money. Curio's task was to block all efforts that Caesar's opponents in the Senate might take to discuss the provincial commands. The young man's ingenuity was equal to the challenge. He proposed a great number of other measures for discussion and used all the parliamentary tactics he could think of to postpone debate on the question of succession in Gaul. Curio's maneuvering succeeded. Events seemed to be working out well for Caesar.

This long-range plan was stymied, however, when the candidate Caesar had supported in the consular election for the year 50 B.C. was defeated. Caesar's enemies were heartened, for they believed he had been dealt a severe blow. They were further encouraged by rumors that the loyalty of his troops, so steady for so long, was wavering.

Caesar, Curio, and the other forces supporting Caesar could, however, take heart from other developments during the year leading up to the crucial election. Marcus Antonius (Mark Antony, as he is generally known), a friend and fellow soldier who had campaigned with Caesar

Vigorous and decisive in his youth, Pompey became less purposeful and more pig-headed as the years passed. He betrayed his former ally Caesar by allowing himself to be cajoled into leading the patrician forces and by refusing to accept a peace when Caesar offered it. In doing so, he made himself morally responsible for the ensuing civil strife.

in Gaul, was elected a tribune for the year 49 B.C. He could be useful to Caesar in that office, as Curio had been. Later in the year, Antony was also elected to fill a vacancy in the College of Augurs, a body of men who interpreted omens on state occasions.

Toward the end of 50 B.C., Caesar decided to cross into Cisalpine Gaul where he would be closer to Rome and better able to exercise control over his affairs. He was still hopeful that he could somehow arrive at an agreement with the Senate that would guarantee him both personal safety and the consulship. In Rome, however, the situation was desperate. Rumors were spreading that Caesar would march into Italy with four legions and that there was little hope of averting civil war. The hostility between the Caesarean faction and the aristocratic party was fast reaching the point where no diplomat could repair the breach.

One of the consuls, Marcellus, called upon Pompey to side openly with Caesar's foes in the dispute. Despite his former alliance with Caesar, Pompey's sympathies were with the patricians. The split between the two men was widened by a new tactic of Curio's. The young tribune suggested that one way to solve the problem facing the state was to have both Pompey and Caesar surrender their commands. Pompey, who had received a five-year command in Spain, could see no reason why he should give up what was legitimately his. The Senate, eager to grasp any· means of avoiding armed conflict, actually approved Curio's proposal, but the measure was later vetoed.

The consul Marcellus finally prevailed upon Pompey to take a definite stand against Caesar and to assume command of the republic's forces in Italy should an invasion by Caesar occur. The Senate also declared that unless Caesar put down his arms by a certain date, he would be considered an outlaw. Now the issue had come to a head. There were last-minute attempts at reconciliation, and messengers sped between Caesar's camp and Rome. But no agreement could be reached. Each side had too great a distrust of the other.

On the night of January 11, 49 B.C., Caesar crossed the Rubicon River, the boundary between Cisalpine Gaul and Italy proper. This crossing amounted to an act of aggression against the state. But Caesar had decided that he must act quickly, even though he had only fifteen hundred

In the miniature at left, Pompey's carriage is pulled into Rome for his second triumph. He was then, at forty-five, Rome's most popular leader. Caesar, on the other hand, only began to win power in middle age (right). Yet Caesar's was the more enduring triumph.

IVLIVS CAESAR

men immediately at hand, rather than allow Pompey time to organize his defenses.

Within days, Caesar's battalions had occupied a number of towns. The garrisons that had been expected to oppose Caesar either joined him or melted away in retreat. Many in Rome were frightened by the ease with which he advanced. Panic seized some in the government as couriers ran into the city with the latest news of Caesar's march. There were even stories that he was about to swoop down upon Rome with his Gallic recruits. This thought was terrifying to the Roman masses, who had never forgotten the Gauls' sack of Rome in 390 B.C.

In this hour of emergency, Pompey decided that his best course would be to evacuate Rome and avoid a fight for the time being. It was the first time in the history of Rome that the city would be abandoned to an enemy, and Pompey's withdrawal intensified the spreading panic. The exodus of government officials was so hurried that there was not time to gather up the money from the treasury.

PALAZZO DEL TE, MANTUA: ALINARI

Among the legends associated with Caesar's crossing of the Rubicon is that he vindictively ordered Pompey's letters and papers destroyed. In reality, the conflict between Caesar and Pompey was political rather than personal.

Even though Pompey had fled, he assumed the role of chief opponent to Caesar. Reports of Caesar's advance and of the increasing disintegration in Rome followed Pompey; the only good news he received during these days was that Labienus, Caesar's skillful adjutant, had left the camp of his commander. There are several possible explanations for his desertion: it could be that Labienus opposed Caesar's defiance of the government; or perhaps Labienus believed that he had not been sufficiently rewarded for his feats in Gaul; or he may have been jealous of the partiality Caesar had shown Antony.

Whatever the reason, an ally of Labienus' skill was welcome in a contest that was to be decided more by might than by right. Yet Pompey's position was perilously insecure. Day by day Caesar advanced, and Pompey retreated down the Italian peninsula. Pompey finally found it prudent to gather his forces at Brindisi, on the Adriatic coast, and ship them from there to Greece. When Caesar arrived at Brindisi, hoping to catch his foe, he found instead that the last of Pompey's troops were sailing out of the harbor. Thus it happened that only sixty-five days after crossing the Rubicon, with a relatively small force, Caesar was master of all of Italy. But he had not been able to arrest Pompey, and the chance for a speedy end to the civil war vanished.

After spending a day or so in Brindisi, Caesar started for Rome. On the way back to the city he had an interview with Cicero and tried, unsuccessfully, to gain the support of the aging statesman whose reputation had not been diminished by Caesar's spectacular accomplishments.

As he neared Rome, Caesar sent an order for all the senators who could be found to assemble and hear his demands. He hoped to persuade them to approve a measure allowing him to take money from the treasury. For if he was to wage a war against Pompey, vast sums would be needed immediately. The Senate approved, and the treasury funds were to be turned over to Caesar. But the Senate's agreement was vetoed by a tribune. Undaunted, Caesar expropriated the money anyway; he even threatened to put the dissenting tribune to death if he interfered, although this official was supposedly inviolable. Such a threat against a tribune confirmed the fear in the hearts of the patricians that Caesar would respect neither law nor man if either one stood in his way.

Now the most important decision facing Caesar was his strategy for continuing the war against Pompey. Since Pompey was on the other side of the Adriatic Sea, Caesar

realized that he presented no immediate danger. So he decided to strike against Pompey's forces in Spain. Before starting out, however, he spent a few days in Rome trying to restore the routine machinery of government so that some order would prevail during his absence. Caesar also ordered Curio to go to Sardinia and Sicily to make sure that the grain supplies Rome depended upon would be safeguarded against possible confiscation by Pompey's forces. With this accomplished, Caesar headed for Spain.

His lieutenant, Fabius, was there waiting for him near the city of Ilerda. Soon after Caesar joined him, the army was nearly trapped by spring floods. But by dint of his own vigor and his engineers' skill, Caesar managed to get his troops to safe ground, and he prepared to pursue the enemy.

Afranius, one of Pompey's commanders in Spain, fell back, but Caesar's well-coordinated advance checked the retreat. After a week of maneuvering, Afranius' supplies failed, and he was soon so short of food and water that he was forced to surrender. Caesar pushed on with such force that in another two months all of Farther Spain was under his control. But his goal there was subjugation rather than vengeance, and he had occasion to show that he could be a magnanimous conqueror. The soldiers he captured were allowed to go free or to join him, as they wished.

On his way back to Rome from Spain, Caesar directed the final assault on the city of Marseilles, which had been under siege for a long time. The satisfaction Caesar received from these successes must have been tempered by the news of the disaster that had overtaken Curio, who had invaded Africa. Curio had been drawn into a trap set by an ally of Pompey named Juba, king of Numidia. Caesar's trusted captain died in the fighting, and only a few of his men survived.

Yet amid the excitement of his forces' triumphs and defeats, Caesar had to concentrate his thoughts on legitimizing his position in the government. The consuls then in office had fled Rome with Pompey, and the normal electoral apparatus of the state could not function. Caesar therefore had a praetor, Lepidus, propose a law creating a dictatorship until the next consular election was held.

Besides their superstitious faith in omens, Romans also believed in a host of supernatural beings— ghosts, demons, goblins, and other spirits both helpful and harmful like the mischievous satyr above.

Romans were governed by omens. Snakes (left, at bottom) were good signs, and good and bad days for business were forecast from the behavior of birds (at top and right). Lightning flashing from right to left, thunderbolts, and eclipses, all bad omens, were reported at the outbreak of the civil war.

Caesar introduced the gold aureus to replace the standard silver denarius, or penny, which had been so debased it was almost valueless. Above is a penny from the reign of Sulla; at top is one of Caesar's.

Caesar, who still intended to run for consul for 48 B.C., had to make sure he held the reins of office securely until then. The role of dictator, which Caesar was granted for the two weeks before the election, gave him the responsibility of conducting the election; equally important, as dictator his acts were immune to a veto by the tribunes.

In those two weeks of supreme power, Caesar accomplished much, particularly on the economic front. The civil war had produced economic chaos and a severe shortage of money. No one was willing to lend capital; business life was almost at a standstill; and debtors found it impossible to pay their bills. Caesar tried to overcome the problem by allowing debtors to meet their obligations by giving up their property, which for these purposes would be estimated at its greater prewar value rather than its current price. Caesar also issued an edict against hoarding, thus putting more money into circulation.

The new dictator was active in other areas as well. He restored civil rights to the descendants of many Romans who had been deprived of their liberties in Sulla's time. He also allowed several exiles to return to Rome. These acts all helped ease fears that Caesar would make revolutionary changes in the state.

At the end of his whirlwind dictatorship, Caesar was elected consul. And he saw to it that his followers filled most of the important posts. Now, securely installed as consul, Caesar could engage Pompey in battle, knowing that the full and legitimate power of Rome was his. Pompey, not Caesar, would be the outlaw fighting against the state.

It has been estimated that Pompey had with him in Greece some 36,000 foot soldiers, 7,000 cavalry, 3,000 archers, and 1,200 slingers. He also had a fleet of 300 ships and large quantities of food and ammunition. But his soldiers, many of them recruits he had gathered during his retreat, were not so battle hardened as Caesar's army of 30,000 men.

Caesar's troops were gathered at Brindisi, but there were not enough ships to carry more than 20,000 men. And since Pompey had so many ships prowling in those waters, a sea crossing was highly dangerous. Nevertheless, Caesar embarked for Greece in January, 48 B.C., leaving orders for Antony and his other commanders to follow him with their men when his ships made the return trip across the Adriatic.

By remarkably good fortune, Caesar's transports managed to avoid Pompey's war galleys. And upon landing on the other side of the Adriatic, Caesar immediately seized several towns. But Pompey's well-executed troop movements prevented Caesar from capturing the more important city of Dyrrachium.

For a while the two armies played a watching game, with Caesar impatiently waiting for the arrival of Antony, who was prevented from sailing by a blockade that had been established by units of Pompey's fleet. Finally, however, Antony slipped clear of the coast of Italy. Though his ships were nearly overtaken by Pompey's galleys, Antony landed safely and soon joined Caesar.

The forces of Caesar and Pompey began to maneuver for better positions. Pompey moved his army so that the sea was at his rear, assuring him of an open supply route. He then built a line of fortifications to protect his front. Caesar, in turn, attempted to enclose the enemy forces between the sea and his own front line.

Brundisium, the modern Brindisi, was the chief Roman port for trade with the East. Below, Pompey's fleet prepares to sail for Illyria as Caesar's men encircle the town.

Seeing the trap, Pompey tried to lure Caesar out of position. He had some of his men make a false offer to Caesar that they would obtain the city of Dyrrachium for him by betrayal. Caesar credulously accepted the offer and led a detachment of soldiers toward the city. Without warning he and his men were ambushed, and a bitter fight ensued in which Caesar nearly lost his life. Simultaneously, Pompey launched two heavy attacks on the center of Caesar's line, but the attack was repulsed. Pompey's next move was to send his soldiers to storm a weak point at a place where Caesar's line approached the sea. There the fighting was at its most furious. The Roman troops panicked when Pompey's men threw back a fresh attack by Caesar, and Caesar was forced to order a retreat.

After some weeks of regrouping, the two armies met again on the plain of Pharsalia during the summer of 48 B.C. Pompey's forces had been heavily reinforced with fresh troops raised by his lieutenant Scipio. However, Pompey was unwilling to engage Caesar in open battle. He was torn by indecision. If he crushed his enemy, posterity would accuse him of the crime of shedding Roman blood.

114

The Battle of Pharsalia is shown as a clash between mounted knights in this stirring and lively panel by a pupil of the painter Uccello.

Caesar had no such scruples and was ready to exploit his enemy's hesitation. For three days Caesar's troops demonstrated on the plain before Pompey's camp in an attempt to lure their foe into action. And for three days Pompey resisted the pleas of his men to attack. But at last his resistance broke, and he yielded. On the fourth morning the two armies marched from their camps and faced each other in what was to be the decisive battle of the civil war (see overleaf).

The Battle of Pharsalia was a catastrophe for Pompey, and he barely managed to escape from the field with his life. Not until seven weeks after Pharsalia was there a report of Pompey; he had turned up off the coast of Egypt, hoping to find asylum there. But, as he stepped ashore, he was brutally assassinated. The Egyptians calculated that killing Pompey was the best way to buy Caesar's favor.

Three days later, when Caesar reached Egypt, he was presented with Pompey's head. It is said that Caesar wept at the sight. Yet with the removal of his chief rival, Caesar's path across the Rubicon and on to the domination of the Roman world seemed to be successfully completed.

THE BATTLE OF PHARSALIA

The three main actions of the Battle of Pharsalia are shown above. The major fighting occurred on the plain at left. Pompey marched out of his camp (left of center) and drew up his infantry, nearly 50,000 strong, with the right flank resting on the Enipeus River, at top. On his left wing he poised his 7,000 cavalrymen, ready to sweep around Caesar's flank and take him in the rear. Caesar, with only 22,000 infantry, relied on a triple line, holding the third in reserve. Backed by a line of six battalions drawn from the reserve (far left), his small force of 1,000 cavalry faced Pompey's.

FRANCIS & SHAW

At the signal Caesar's first lines charged and locked with the main force of the enemy. At once Pompey's cavalry went into action, driving back Caesar's squadrons, but they were routed in turn by the six battalions. They fled into the hills (at bottom). Pompey, seeing this, returned to his camp. The victorious six battalions, meanwhile, wheeled to take the enemy on the flank, and Caesar immediately threw in his reserves. Pompey's line crumbled and fell back on its camp. But Caesar's men could not be stopped; they stormed the position, and the garrison took refuge on the surround-ing heights as Pompey fled for the coast. Without water, the survivors left the hills and began a retreat west along a ridge leading to the river. Caesar followed with four legions, and toward evening brought the last of Pompey's men to bay on a plateau at the river's edge (far right). The next morning, unable to descend to the river or to escape, they surrendered. The battle was over, but the cost in Roman lives was heavy. For, al-though Caesar lost only 200 legionaries and 30 centurions, 15,000 of Pompey's once-proud army were captives, and 25,000 more lay dead on the plain of Pharsalia.

VII

HAIL, CAESAR!

This bronze of Cleopatra is a reliable portrait, bearing a marked resemblance to those on her coins.

More by accident than design, Caesar arrived in Egypt at a most opportune time. He disembarked at the city of Alexandria with a small, elite force of twelve hundred men in the midst of a struggle for power between the members of Egypt's royal house. Three years earlier the ruler of Egypt had died, leaving as co-rulers his daughter Cleopatra and his young son Ptolemy. Each had a group of crafty advisers who were scheming to oust the other from the throne. Several months before Caesar landed in Egypt, Ptolemy's supporters had managed to force Cleopatra from the country. But she had promptly raised an army and was preparing to return to Egypt to fight for the throne.

Hearing that Caesar had established himself and his soldiers in the royal palace and that he had announced his decision to appoint a ruler for Egypt, Cleopatra made plans to reach him and present her case. Legend has it that one night a small boat slipped out of the Mediterranean blackness past Alexandria's lighthouse, which stood sentinel-like before the city, and glided into the harbor. The boat, sculled by a single man, neared a broad flight of steps that came down to the water from the palace and other public buildings. Shouldering a rolled-up carpet such as travelers often used to carry their belongings, the man stepped out of the boat, walked up the steps, and asked to be taken to Caesar. Once in Caesar's presence, the man unbound the carpet—and out stepped Cleopatra.

She was an ambitious and spirited young woman who had just reached the age of twenty-one. As she pleaded her cause with wit and passion, Caesar found himself attracted to her. He decided that he and his soldiers would give her

In the first-century Roman mosaic at left, the Nile River flows placidly past an ancient Egyptian temple. At top, Nubian hunters pursue a leopard, and at bottom Roman legionaries carouse beside Egypt's life-giving river.

protection in the palace until he could secure her place on the throne.

However, Caesar's position in Alexandria was dangerous. He had troops enough to defend the palace but not to gain control of the harbor and its approaches. He had called for reinforcements, but until they arrived he had to depend on his wits and the loyalty of his men. The population of the city was hostile to him because it resented the way he, a Roman, assumed he could dispose of Egypt's future. He had incurred the hatred of Ptolemy's advisers for siding with Cleopatra, and they began to plot against him. Arsinoë, Cleopatra's younger sister, was also eager for power. She slipped out of the palace and joined Caesar's opponents. In addition, Caesar allowed Cleopatra's brother to leave the palace, where he had been detained. Perhaps Caesar hoped that this would produce a struggle for leadership between Cleopatra's rivals—any dissension in the enemy camp would help him in his unequal struggle to bind the country to Rome.

In the months that followed, the forces of Ptolemy and

Arsinoë made repeated attempts to drive Caesar and Cleopatra from the palace. Once, the Egyptians polluted Caesar's water supply, but he set his men to digging, and they uncovered a fresh source of water. On another occasion, Caesar made a sudden foray out of the palace and seized a strategic part of Pharos Island, on which the lighthouse stood. This opened his way to the sea, giving him a route through which reinforcements could come or by which he could escape if necessary. On still another day, Caesar attempted to seize the pier that connected Pharos with the mainland, but he was beaten off and had to swim for his life.

As the reinforcements for which Caesar had sent began to arrive, his situation improved considerably. He was now able to control the harbor and the city. One relief force of Syrian and Cilician allies was fighting its way down the Nile toward Alexandria. Ptolemy's generals hoped to crush this army, but luckily Caesar was informed of their plan in time, and he set out with a major portion of his army to support the relieving troops. In a sharp battle, his forces defeated and routed the army of Ptolemy, and the royal youth himself was killed. Caesar returned to Cleopatra with the welcome news that her brother and many of her enemies were dead; her rule in Egypt was now uncontested.

Cleopatra readily agreed to have Arsinoë sent to Italy for safekeeping. Then, she and Caesar, whose affection for each other had matured in the weeks of crisis, departed from Alexandria for a leisurely cruise up the Nile. It was a cruise without any equal for sumptuousness: the

A Macedonian general founded the dynasty of Ptolemies — from which Cleopatra came — when he usurped the throne of Egypt in the fourth century B.C. The new Pharaohs, although not Egyptian, maintained the customs and styles of the ancient kings. The mummy at left was entombed in about 100 A.D., and the sphinx at right — ancient symbol of royal authority — was carved for a Ptolemy in the third century B.C. Their temple of Hathor (above) at Dendera was still under construction when Caesar landed in Egypt.

royal boat is said to have been made of cedar and cyprus and decorated with gold leaf; on its decks were dining salons and parlors, all richly furnished; and a crew of specially selected slaves rowed the boat gently through the water. In other, somewhat less elegant, river vessels, generals, retainers, and servants trailed the royal barge. A broad desert sky by night, a brilliant sun by day, the history of ancient Egypt spelling out its tale in the monuments by the side of the river—it was indeed a splendid journey.

But now, by the spring of 47 B.C., Caesar could ignore the affairs of Rome no longer. After returning to Alexandria, he went to Asia Minor where he reorganized the provincial administration and distributed certain lands to reward allies. As a special compensation for aiding him in the Egyptian campaign, he exempted the Jewish people from having to provide winter quarters for his troops.

In this theatre, Caesar's main task was to deal with Pharnaces, the son of Mithridates, who was attempting to enlarge his kingdom by annexing new lands in eastern Asia Minor. Caesar joined his army near the border of Pontus and marched to meet Pharnaces. As the armies neared each other, Pharnaces decided upon a sudden at-

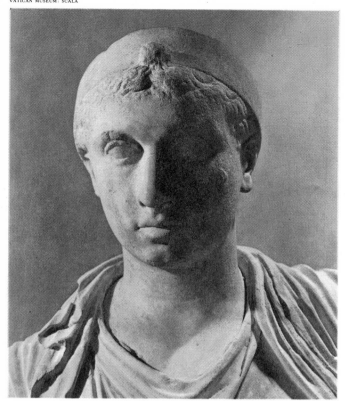

On the panel below, the Renaissance artist de Landi depicted Cleopatra as a woman of his own time. She is shown seated in the stern of a ship that is nearing the coast of Asia Minor on the way to Rome. The portraits of her at left and at far left below were carved by a Roman sculptor who has portrayed the queen as more Greek looking than Egyptian.

123

The following labels appear on the map:

BRITAIN

Thames R.

ENGLISH CHANNEL

● Boulogne

ATUATUCI
NERVII

Rhine R.

VENETI

BELGAE

ATLANTIC OCEAN

Loire R.

● Bourges ● Alesia ● Besançon
● Geneva
● Gergovia HELVETII

AEDUI

CISALPINE
GAUL

Rhone R.

TRANSALPINE GAUL

● Luca

Rubicon R.

ADRIATIC SEA

● Marseilles
Narbonne

SPAIN

ILLYRIA

● Ilerda

● ROME

● Dyrrachium

ITALY

MACEDONIA

● Munda

BALEARIC
ISLANDS

● Brindisi

● Pharsalus

● Cadiz

● Mytilene

MEDITERRANEAN SEA

SICILY

GREECE

RHODI

● Thapsus

CRETE

NUMIDIA

AFRICA

ASI

**THE ROMAN EMPIRE
IN THE TIME OF
JULIUS CAESAR**

tack. But Caesar was not caught off guard; after hours of hard fighting, the battle turned against Pharnaces, and he was forced to flee. The young leader was killed a short time later. In a dispatch to Rome, Caesar summed up the brief campaign with the words *"Veni, Vidi, Vici"*—"I came, I saw, I conquered."

Caesar finally returned to Rome in the summer of 47 B.C., after an absence of more than a year and a half. During most of that time, Rome had been ruled by Antony, who, acting for Caesar, had shown a typical lack of good judgment. Public order had broken down while he amused himself with his disreputable friends. Gangs had fought in the streets, as they had in Clodius' day. When an impoverished young tribune had proposed the abolition of debts and rents, the poor people of Rome rioted in support of the measure, and Antony had to restore order with force.

Caesar quickly took charge. He canceled rents that were less than a certain maximum, thus alleviating some of the financial stress. He filled the ranks of the depleted Senate to make that body function effectively once more, and he had himself elected consul for the year 46 B.C. While working at restoring order in Rome, he was faced with an even more difficult situation outside the city.

Caesar's veteran troops stationed near Rome were restless, and they could not be restrained from demanding the reward promised them for their long labors. They marched on the city and camped outside the walls, where Caesar finally appeared before them. He told the troops he would discharge them and meet their requests, and he addressed them as "citizens," indicating that he no longer considered them under his command. To be dismissed in this way was too much of a humiliation for his men to bear. "They could endure it no longer," the Roman historian Appian wrote, "but cried out that they had repented of what they had done, and besought him to keep them in his service. But Caesar turned away and was leaving the platform when they shouted with greater eagerness and urged him to stay and punish the guilty among them."

Caesar finally said that he would not punish anyone. But he added that for taking part in the disturbances, the Tenth Legion, to which he had always shown such honor, would be dismissed without a hearing. The men of the Tenth Legion felt they had been stripped to their very souls, and they begged Caesar to condemn some of them by lot, and put those soldiers to death, while pardoning the rest. "But Caesar," Appian relates, "seeing that there was no need of stimulating them any further when they repented so bitterly, became reconciled to all and departed straightway for the war in Africa." With such political melodrama, Caesar was able to stay on top of his tumultuous times and survive for the next encounter.

It was in Africa that Caesar's enemies—Labienus, Afranius, Cato, two of Pompey's sons, and other malcontents— had gathered with some 35,000 men and considerable cavalry. There were also the allied armies of Juba, the mighty king of Numidia, with whom Caesar had to contend.

Caesar sailed for the southern coast of the Mediterranean in October 47 B.C., knowing only that it would be a fierce campaign that either side could win. For Caesar's forces were inferior in number: his army comprised no more than six legions, and most of these troops were raw recruits. The enemy, on the other hand, was numerous, and its positions were in fortified towns, well supplied and well located. Therefore, after landing in Africa, Caesar spent some time training the recruits and waiting for the arrival of reinforcements, which would include many of his veterans.

In due time additional forces did arrive, and Caesar marched in strength to the city of Thapsus. The approaches to the city were over two narrow pieces of land on either side of a body of water. Scipio, the commander of the enemy troops in Thapsus, tried to trap Caesar on one of the isthmuses, but in doing so only succeeded in trapping himself. When Caesar's bottled-up men charged to defend themselves, Scipio found that the land was too narrow to permit an orderly retreat to safety. His army was slain to the last man.

Before many weeks had passed, Caesar controlled all of Roman Africa. The news of Scipio's defeat at Thapsus had sapped the will of some to resist Caesar; others thought it would be wiser to fight elsewhere. The disposition of the African alliance was swift: Labienus and Pompey's sons

GOODENOUGH, *Jewish Symbols in the Greco-Roman Period*, BY PERMISSION OF THE BOLLINGEN FOUNDATION

Jewish troops, like the squad of legionaries at left, helped to rescue Caesar from his perilous position in Alexandria. As a reward, Jerusalem was not occupied by Roman legions. Other Mediterranean nations were not so fortunate. In many places, ruins such as those above at Dougga, Tunisia, bear silent witness to centuries of continuous occupation by the Romans.

The civil war in Africa virtually ended at Thapsus (above) when the Pompeians (left) were wiped out by Caesar's outnumbered army (center). Caesar's men, anxious to finish the war and go home, charged the Pompeians against his orders.

escaped to Spain; Afranius fell into Caesar's hands and was executed without further ceremony. Juba had a Roman colleague kill him when his capital city closed its gates to him and would not let him enter; and Cato, in charge of the defense of the city of Utica, fell on his own sword.

Whereas the conquest of Gaul had established Caesar's reputation, and the victory at Pharsalia had eliminated Caesar's chief rival, the slaughter at Thapsus, and its aftereffects, made him supreme in the Mediterranean world. All Rome rushed to pay homage to him. The Senate, not wanting to offend Caesar with any paltry honors, ordered a thanksgiving of forty days. At last the time was at hand when Caesar could reap the harvest of his long labors in Gaul, Spain, Asia, and Africa. He began by celebrating triumphal processions such as had never before been seen in Rome.

On the day of the first triumph, the streets of Rome were

EROS
OMNIA PER...
AMANVS
FRVNITVS

The Roman way of life soon spread through the conquered lands, often replacing the native cultures. The fine mosaic of a charioteer above, though typically Roman in subject and style, was made by a Tunisian artist in the second century A.D.

garlanded with flowers. Throughout the city, altars were ablaze with burning incense. The crowd was thick along the parade route—many of those in the front rows had spent a good part of the night there to be sure of getting a fine view. At last the signal was given for the commencement of the procession. Heading the parade were the city magistrates; then, less sedately, came the trumpeters. They were followed by a long line of wagons and chariots loaded with displays of all the treasures taken in the Gallic wars. Men carried signs lettered with the names of defeated nations and of the towns where Caesar had won his greatest victories. Paintings and other works of art, which Caesar had commissioned for the occasion, depicted notable events in the struggle for Gaul.

An impressive retinue of priests appeared next. Then came the animals to be sacrificed to the gods. There were human sacrifices too: captive kings and chieftains walked blinking in the sunlight after long imprisonment in the

Vercingetorix (above) died at the executioner's hands after he had been dragged through the streets of Rome for Caesar's first triumph.

dungeons of Rome. And Vercingetorix, a prisoner since his surrender, was there, along with other Gallic leaders whose lives would soon be taken. There were musicians, an honor guard—and finally the chariot of Caesar himself came into view. Behind Caesar marched his men, proud of their achievements and warmed by the acclaim.

A few days later, Caesar celebrated a second triumph. This one commemorated his Egyptian victory. One of the spectators was Cleopatra, who had come to Rome at Caesar's invitation. She was able to watch her own sister, Arsinoë, whom she continued to hate, walking in chains as a prisoner of Caesar's.

Yet a third triumph celebrated the victory over Pharnaces. And a fourth triumph was held for the victory in North Africa. Caesar had a problem in this case. He did not care to remind Romans of his victory over fellow Romans. So the triumph ostensibly celebrated the annexation of the kingdom of Numidia.

This was only the beginning. Caesar was the host at a public banquet for the poor at which there was supposed

The pageantry and splendor of Caesar's triumphs surpassed anything Rome had seen before. Above, in a panel by a fifteenth-century Italian painter,

130

to have been some twenty thousand people. Every guest received a cash gift, grain, and quantities of oil for lighting their homes.

Then he turned to his veterans. With the generosity of the astute politician, he assigned to them lands that had been provided by the state. Every soldier also received the long-promised bonuses. Then, realizing that his strength was based on the army command system, as well as on the popular will, Caesar awarded even larger sums to his invaluable centurions. All officers ultimately received proportionately greater benefits than did the common soldiers.

Every part of the city was swept up in the excitement. A big-game hunt in one of the stadia featured four hundred lions. Sporting events of every sort were staged in all the arenas, and theatrical performances in many languages were given. There was a sham naval battle on an artificial lake, and a mock land battle. Had they not been rather used to the displays of free-spending politicians, the Roman people might have exhausted themselves just running from one event to another. "Such a throng flocked to all those

sacrificial animals and a cart loaded with plunder (center), followed by a float carrying a statue of the triumphant Caesar, enter the gates of Rome.

shows from every quarter," Suetonius wrote, "that many strangers had to lodge in tents pitched in the streets or along the roads, and the press was often such that many, including two senators, were crushed to death."

But neither Rome nor Caesar could enjoy his triumphs for long. Only a few months after these extravagant festivities, the unvanquished remnants of the Pompeian party in Spain renewed their war against Caesar. None of the loyal commanders in Spain was able to defeat the rebels, who were headed by Labienus and Pompey's sons. So once again Caesar took to the field. In November 46 B.C., he left Rome for the last military campaign of his life.

For months after arriving in Spain, Caesar pushed the enemy back without finding an opportunity for a decisive battle. Finally, in northern Spain, outside the town of Munda, the two armies faced each other. The Pompeians had the advantage of holding a position on a hill from which they charged when Caesar approached. Hours passed as the two evenly matched armies fought, but gradually the up-hill fighting began to tire Caesar's men. Caesar himself rushed into the thick of the battle to rally his troops. Their commander beside them, their spirits rose, and one of the legions pushed back the enemy's left flank. Caesar now called for his cavalry to strike at the enemy's other flank. Labienus, observing Caesar's move, withdrew some of his soldiers and hurried them behind his lines to reinforce the men facing Caesar's charge. Labienus' legionaries, seeing this movement, believed it was the beginning of a retreat. Their lines broke, and as they fled, they were ridden down and killed by Caesar's troops. Labienus, who had fought so long for Caesar, died on the field of battle fighting against him. With the destruction of the Pompeian army in Spain, the civil war was finally ended.

Caesar journeyed back to Rome honored and acclaimed as no Roman had ever been. The state offered him the most extraordinary powers and privileges—he was to be dictator for ten years and was to have the right to nominate candidates for key offices. Magistrates henceforth would be obliged to swear not to oppose any of his decrees. Even more extraordinary, the person of Caesar was declared inviolable. As if he were larger than life, statues of Caesar

In Tiepolo's painting at left, Cleopatra enters Rome with fitting ceremony, for as queen of Egypt she was honored as a goddess. After his death, Caesar was also deified; the coin above reads CAESAR DIVI.F, "Divine Caesar."

In a series of tumultuous canvases, the excitement of Caesar's triumph was recaptured by Mantegna. Above, soldiers stagger under trophies of looted arms and treasure.

appeared everywhere. Temples were dedicated to him. And it was decreed that the month of Quintilis, his birth month, would hereafter be known as Julius.

There were some among the senatorial groups who hoped that Caesar would give up his uncommon powers and rule within the limits of the constitution. There were many, on the other hand, who feared the worst and still expected a rash of revolutionary pronouncements. Caesar, however, had no intention either of giving up the power he had attained or of overturning the established order.

Much of the legislation he would propose, or would

The chariot, regarded as a vehicle only for kings, was forbidden in republican Rome except to a general on the day of his triumph. Above, Caesar, crowned, rides in splendor.

have others propose for him, before 45 B.C., was aimed at eliminating injustices perpetrated by the middle classes against the masses. His efforts to relieve debtors, his extension of the right to vote to the Cisalpine Gauls and others, his crack-down on corrupt electoral practices, were all acts of a man interested in preserving stability and establishing a framework for government.

For these and other efforts he would win wide backing among the people. But he could never win the loyalty of the aristocracy—and in the end it was the aristocracy that brought him down.

THE IDES OF MARCH

Upon his return to Rome in 45 B.C., Caesar plunged into affairs of state with the same lightning energy and whirl-wind effectiveness that had characterized his military career. In all the administrative reforms he issued, he tried to make his personal rule more solid and more direct. He reorganized the government and administration of the towns in Italy. He established a system of customs dues in an attempt to regulate the amount of money coming into the treasury. He limited the governorship in consular provinces to two years. He also amended the criminal law so that in all Roman territories crimes of violence would be punishable by severe penalties.

Having disposed of these organizational problems, Caesar turned to the political front. There he forged ahead with little concern for precedents or for what others might prefer. He abolished the political clubs, known as *collegia*, which had so often been used as weapons of violence at election time and on other critical occasions when mob action might affect the government. He ordered laws to be passed chastising the aristocracy: one of these limited the degree of ostentation and luxury that might be displayed. And he put through a bill that provided jobs for veterans.

Not content with limiting his lawmaking to government and politics, Caesar moved into the realm of the arts and sciences. He ordered that the Roman calendar year, which was only 355 days, be lengthened to 365 1/4 days. (Prior to this it had been the Roman habit to insert an extra month in a year when the seasons were obviously out of date.) Statutes were prepared for the control of traffic, the upkeep of the roads in Rome, the utilization of open spaces, and the supervision of the grain supply. He also projected vast engineering schemes to drain marshes, to build a road across the Apennines to the Adriatic Sea, to deepen the harbor near Rome, to dig a new channel for the Tiber River and so be able to control its waters. He made plans

The common people raised Caesar to power and were rewarded by the new laws he made for their benefit. This mural shows a group of typical plebeians.

The device at left calculates the phases of the moon for any year by means of a rotating center piece. But the old Roman calendar gave the year only 355 days, so no astronomical device could make time in Rome correspond to time kept by the moon or planets. By 45 B.C. the calendar was 67 days ahead of the real date. Caesar ordered the Greek mathematician Sosigenes to draw up a new and accurate calendar based on the work of Egyptian astronomers. This Julian calendar, named for Caesar, is in use today.

to build public libraries and theatres, to raise a temple to the god Mars, and to codify the civil law.

Some of these projects would have to wait, however, until Caesar carried out his most ambitious military plan— a massive expedition against the kingdom of Parthia. It would be an opportunity for Rome to avenge herself for the death of Crassus, and the riches of Parthia would make a welcome addition to the Roman treasury. But perhaps the most compelling reason, in Caesar's mind, was a personal one—his health had not been good. Straining to keep all the controls of Rome's government in his hands had apparently tired him greatly; he may have looked forward to the rigorous but less complicated demands of a military campaign. Whatever his inward thoughts, he ordered that an armada of unprecedented size be assembled and made ready to sail to the East.

Yet neither Caesar's plans for a great military campaign nor his personal popularity impressed his old enemies. Each new ordinance and each new project, no matter how moderate or beneficent, was resented by the conservative classes. Their hostility toward Caesar was at first a matter of suspicion and petty annoyance: a number of senators were dismayed at the loss of personal privileges; others were angered by the presence of Cleopatra in Rome; and still others were upset by the triumph Caesar celebrated after his last victory in Spain—which had been over Romans. But annoyance among the conservatives soon changed to deep concern as they realized the immense power Caesar had gathered to himself.

All their lives Romans had been taught to believe in the soundness of a republican government in which every issue affecting the state could be brought to a vote in the Senate or the People's Assembly. The government was supposed to exist as an instrument of the people's decisions. Now that the government merely served to carry out Caesar's will, the vital popular rights of voting and electing were decaying from lack of use.

The bronze tablet below records a measure introduced by Caesar. It defines the rules of procedure and the areas of jurisdiction for the local courts in Cisalpine Gaul.

It even occurred to observers that Caesar wanted to be recognized as a king—that he would force Rome to become a monarchy once again, as it had been centuries before. Indeed there were a few signs that he considered himself a king already. When addressed by some senators, he chose not to rise from his seat—an apparent admission that he did not consider them his equals, but his inferiors. One day a statue of Caesar was found to be adorned with a diadem, the emblem of royalty. The tribunes Marullus and Flavus ordered the mysterious diadem to be removed. On another occasion, in January 44 B.C., someone in a crowd hailed Caesar as king, but Caesar, showing no displeasure, silenced the voice.

The next month, Caesar was reviewing a procession from a platform. One of his followers, probably Antony, put a crown on Caesar's head. Caesar took it off. Again the crown was placed on his head, and again Caesar removed it. He ordered, however, that it be inscribed in the official records that the people had offered him a crown and that he had refused it.

Perhaps the rumors that Caesar desired to have himself declared king were merely the stories of enemies in the Senate. Perhaps their keen resolve to stop the erosion of their aristocratic rights convinced them of the truth of the stories being circulated. And perhaps the echoes of their own stories and the horror of the very possibility of monarchy persuaded them that there was only one way to stop the dictator—by assassination.

A senator named Gaius Cassius, a man who had been on Pompey's side in the civil war but whom Caesar had pardoned after the Battle of Pharsalia, was apparently the one who first began sounding out other senators. Soon, at least sixty indicated that they approved of Cassius' plan of assassination.

Included in this group was Marcus Brutus, who some thought was Caesar's illegitimate son, and to whom Caesar had always shown particular favor. At the Battle of Pharsalia, for instance, Caesar had given specific orders that young Brutus—who had sided with Pompey—was not to be harmed. Brutus, in the opinion of some historians, was a weak and bookish man, but he was apparently a good and kind human being as well. He enjoyed great prestige in Rome, and the conspirators believed their deed would win more immediate popular favor if Brutus was one of them.

The date for the assassination was fixed for March 15,

VATICAN MUSEUM, ROME: ALINARI

These golden diadems, shaped like garlands, were only used by the Romans to crown ancestral statues.

140

The Romans abhorred the idea of kingship: the central figure in the stage
painting above is a tragic king; beside him a girl regards a mask of horror.

142

when the Senate was due to assemble, and just a day or two before Caesar intended to depart for the Parthian campaign. The plan was simple. Each conspirator would come to the Senate that day with a dagger concealed beneath his toga. At a given signal a group of them would throw themselves at Caesar and stab him. The act would be carried out in full sight of the entire Senate—thus making it appear not as a sinister murder, but as a deed honorably done for the sake and safety of the state.

On the night of March 14, Caesar gathered with some friends, perhaps to discuss final arrangements for his campaign and to take care of last-minute details pertaining to the administration of Rome in his absence. The men began discussing death and what might be the best kind of death. "A sudden one," Caesar is reported to have said.

The next morning, his wife, Calpurnia, begged Caesar not to go to the Senate that day. She said she had dreamed terrible things and feared something monstrous was going to happen. Caesar, though unaffected by his wife's pleas, apparently felt slightly indisposed, and he decided not to go to the Senate building after all.

For the conspirators, however, it was too late to withdraw; each one of them had passed his own private Rubicon of decision. And as each one walked or was borne by litter to the appointed assembly point he must have reconsidered why he had determined that Caesar must die. Certainly, Caesar had ridden over many of the republic's most cherished institutions and had alienated the Senate by ignoring many of its ancient privileges. But Caesar had also won Gaul and had secured for the Romans rich territories on other continents. He was Rome's greatest military genius, as well as an inspired popular leader who had given the state much well-applied legislation that was badly needed. More than a statesman, he was now the state— and it was that fact in particular that the patricians could not tolerate.

As had been so carefully planned, the conspirators assembled, expecting the arrival of Caesar momentarily. And there they waited until late in the morning. Why had Caesar not come? Did he suspect something? Decimus Brutus, a conspirator, went to Caesar's house to see what

Michelangelo made the bust of Brutus at left. It bears a striking resemblance to the head of Brutus on the coin above, at top, which commemorates the death of Caesar. The reverse of the coin shows the assassins' daggers.

was happening. He derided Calpurnia's fears, perhaps hinting that it was not proper for a man such as Caesar to be influenced by a woman's dreams. He finally prevailed upon Caesar, who was feeling better, to change his mind and come to the Senate as planned.

As Caesar stepped from his litter before the Senate building, a friend handed him a note, imploring Caesar to read it instantly. But the crush of the people was so great, Caesar had no chance to do so. Just before he entered the Senate building, he saw a soothsayer who had warned him some time before to beware of the ides of March, the fifteenth of the month. "The ides of March have come," Caesar said. "But not gone," the soothsayer replied.

Although historical sources disagree on precisely what happened next, the general outline is clear. As Caesar crossed the threshold, Antony began to follow but was detained in conversation by a conspirator. It had been agreed that only Caesar must be struck down, no one else.

Inside, Caesar walked to his seat. A small group of men came forward. One of them, Tillius Cimber, begged Caesar to recall his brother from exile. Caesar refused. Cimber implored, pressing close upon Caesar. Caesar asked him to stand back. Instead Cimber caught hold of Caesar's toga and pulled it roughly back, leaving the dictator's neck and chest exposed.

It was the signal for murder. Casca, a friend of Cassius, struck with his dagger but managed to inflict only a slight wound. Caesar fought back. The others attacked him. For a few moments Caesar struggled with his assailants. When he saw that Brutus too was coming toward him with dagger in hand, he stopped fighting. As Brutus stabbed him, Caesar covered his face with his toga, and staggering to the foot of a statue of Pompey, fell and died.

As Caesar fell there were wild outcries from the rest of the Senate. The senators rushed from the hall. When the assassins emerged, still holding their bloody daggers, the people fled through the streets in terror. That night, and for weeks after, the city was wracked by riots. Surely not one of the conspirators could have imagined how widespread the consequences of his action would be.

After the first shock of Caesar's death wore off, Antony attempted to seize power by himself, but he was unable to buy or bully his way into Caesar's role. Then Antony formed a triumvirate with Octavian, who was Caesar's nephew and principal heir, and Lepidus, who had once served as consul with Caesar. The first item on their pro-

TEXT CONTINUED ON PAGE 148

Caesar's assassination fascinated men of the Renaissance, to whom such a crime was unthinkable. The events of the fatal day are shown in two Renaissance works at right. Below, Caesar is borne on a litter to the Senate as Spurina the soothsayer (center), with arms upraised, utters his dire warning. At right, Caesar is murdered by Brutus and his co-conspirator Cassius as Brutus' wife, Porcia, faints in horror.

144

BOCCACIO, *De Claris Mulieribus*, 1473

HISTORICAL MUSEUM, BEF

145

THE CHALLENGE OF CAESAR

The towering figure of Julius Caesar has loomed as a challenge to artists across many centuries. Rubens, who made the pen drawing opposite, saw him as the man of war, crowned with a victor's laurels. A fifteenth-century sculptor—some say Donatello—who carved the bas-relief below at right portrayed the dictator, his face scarred by the responsibilities of office. Among the writers, Shakespeare, in his play *Julius Caesar*, based on the works of Plutarch, made him a ruthless tyrant. In the illustration from a 1709 edition of the play below at left, Brutus, in the foreground, hovers over Caesar's dead body. Yet, although the complex personality of the man has inspired many fine works of art in many styles and mediums, no one, not even the greatest, has ever been able to capture completely the spirit of this extraordinary personage.

Caesar's death mask is at left. Masks of molded wax, which were made for aristocratic and wealthy Romans soon after they died, were used in several ways. At funerals an actor wore the dead man's mask in the procession, and a cast made from it preceded the bier. Afterward, the family placed it with the other ancestral masks displayed in the entrance hall of their house to serve as a model for portraits. Many of the portraits of Caesar that appear in this book were copied from the mask at left.

TEXT CONTINUED FROM PAGE 144

gram—whether out of love for Caesar or to preserve their own political skins—was to avenge the assassination. The Triumvirate ordered the execution of several thousand Romans, including the venerable Cicero. Brutus and Cassius, fighting in the name of the republic, committed suicide in 42 B.C. as their armies were being defeated by Antony.

But the blood bath that began to be drawn with Caesar's death would not be full until the wars of the rivals raged the breadth of the Mediterranean and the length of Italy. Both Antony and Cleopatra met violent deaths, as did every other major actor in the great drama of Caesar's Rome—some in war, some in flight, some by suicide.

Only Octavian remained. He chose to call himself Augustus—"exalted"—and as the sole possessor of the Roman world, the name was apt. Behind Augustus lay the republic's bloody end; ahead of him stretched the glorious future of the empire that Caesar had brought into being.

Caesar's successors, three of whom appear in this cameo, completed the work he had begun. At top, Augustus, Caesar's heir and Rome's first emperor, rides Pegasus. At center, Tiberius, Augustus' successor, holds the imperial scepter, which passed to his grandson Caligula, who stands at far left.

149

Caesar, mounted at right, rides triumphantly into Rome behind the eagle standard.

AMERICAN HERITAGE PUBLISHING CO., INC.

James Parton, *President*

Joseph J. Thorndike, Jr., *Editor in Chief*

Richard M. Ketchum, *Editorial Director, Book Division*

Irwin Glusker, *Art Director*

HORIZON CARAVEL BOOKS

RUSSELL BOURNE, *Managing Editor*

Sean Morrison, *Assistant Editor*

Janet Czarnetzki, *Art Director*

Judith Harkison, *Chief Picture Researcher*

Lucy Davidson Rosenfeld, *Picture Researcher*

Elaine K. Andrews, *Copy Editor*

Nancy Simon, *Editorial Assistant*

Betsy Sanders, *Editorial Assistant*

Gertrudis Feliu, *Chief, European Bureau*

Claire de Forbin, *European Bureau*

ACKNOWLEDGMENTS

The Editors are deeply grateful to the curators of many museums and private collections in the United States and Europe for their help in making available material of special interest to this book. Special thanks are owed to Maria Todorow, Ann Natanson, Bianca Spantigati, and Fiorella Ginanneschi for their assistance and research in Italy, to Susanne Puddefoot in England, and to the following individuals and organizations for their generous cooperation:

Bollingen Foundation, New York

Dr. Raymond V. Schoder, S.J.

Dr. Joseph W. Owen, New York

Hofrat DDr. Franz Unterkircher, Director of Manuscripts Department, Austrian National Library, Vienna

Mrs. Gay M. Herzman, North Carolina Museum of Art

Dr. Eric Young and Mrs. Elaine Evans, Egyptology Department, The Metropolitan Museum of Art

Prof. R. Laur-Belart, Curator, Romerhaus und Museum, Augst, Switzerland

Allen D. Wassall, Director, John Woodman Higgins Armory, Worcester, Mass.

Dr. Pietrangeli, Capitoline Museum, Rome

Mr. M. Temmam, Curator, Musée des Antiquités Classiques et Musulmanes, Algiers

Oliver Millar, Deputy Surveyor of the Queen's Pictures and The Comptroller, Lord Chamberlain's Office, St. James's Palace, London

John C. Simmons, Entertainments and Publicity Manager, Borough of Deal, Kent, England

The Science Museum, London

Departments of Greek and Roman Antiquities, British and Medieval Antiquities, Coins and Medals, and Printed Books, British Museum

Special drawings by Sean Morrison

150

FURTHER REFERENCE

Readers interested in further viewing examples of art and armament from the time of Julius Caesar will find exhibitions of Roman antiquities in many American museums. Foremost among the collections of art from Rome and the Roman world are those in The Metropolitan Museum of Art, New York City; the Santa Barbara Museum of Art; the William Rockhill Nelson Gallery of Art, Kansas City; the John Woodman Higgins Armory, Worcester, Mass.; the Kelsey Museum of Archaeology, University of Michigan; and the Museum of Fine Arts, Boston.

For those who wish to read further on Caesar and Roman civilization, the following books are recommended:

Caesar, Gaius Julius. *War Commentaries*. Ed. & Trans. by John Warrington. Dutton Everyman, 1958.

Carcopino, Jerome. *Daily Life in Ancient Rome*. Yale Univ. Press, 1958.

Cowell, F. R. *The Revolutions of Ancient Rome*. Frederick A. Praeger, 1962.

Dickinson, John. *Death of a Republic*. The Macmillan Co., 1963.

Dudley, Donald R. *The Civilization of Rome*. Mentor Book, 1960.

Ferrero, Guglielmo. *The Life of Caesar*. W. W. Norton & Co., 1962.

Grant, Michael. *The World of Rome*. The World Publ. Co., 1960.

Grimal, Pierre. *The Civilization of Rome*. Simon and Schuster, 1963.

Haywood, Richard M. *Myth of Rome's Fall*. Thomas Y. Crowell Co., 1958.

Kahler, Heinz. *The Art of Rome and Her Empire*. Crown Publishers, Inc., 1963.

Maiuri, Amedeo. *Roman Painting*. Skira, n.d.

Mommsen, Theodor. *The History of Rome*. Meridian Books, 1961.

Nash, Ernest. *Pictorial Dictionary of Ancient Rome*. 2 vols. Frederick A. Praeger, 1961.

Oman, Charles. *Seven Roman Statesmen*. Edward Arnold & Co., 1957.

Plutarch. *The Lives of the Noble Grecians and Romans*. The Modern Library, n.d.

Pobe, Marcel. *The Art of Roman Gaul*. Univ. of Toronto Press, 1961.

Scherer, Margaret R. *Marvels of Ancient Rome*. The Phaidon Press for The Metropolitan Museum of Art, 1955.

Seyffert, Oscar. *Dictionary of Classical Antiquities*. Meridian Books, 1956.

Stenico, Arturo. *Roman and Etruscan Painting*. Compass History of Art, 1963.

Stobart, J. C. *The Grandeur That Was Rome*. Hawthorn Books, 1961.

The Cambridge Ancient History. *The Roman Republic*. Vol. IX. Cambridge Univ. Press, 1951.

Tranquillus, Gaius Suetonius. *The Twelve Caesars*. Penguin Books, 1957.

INDEX

Bold face indicates pages on which maps or illustrations appear

Adriatic Sea, 58, 109, 112, 113, 137
Afranius, 111, 125, 128
Africa, 12, 13, 40, 111, 125–128
Aisne River, 69, 70
Alesia, siege of, 92, **92–93,** 94–95, **94–95,** 98, **98,** 99
Alexandria, Egypt, 119, 120, 121, 122, 127
Ambiorix, 82, **82–83,** 88, **88–89,** 92
Antonine Column, **67**
Antony, Mark (Marcus Antonius), 104, **104,** 105, 109, 112, 113, 124, 125, 140, 144, 148
Apennines (mountain range), 137
Appian, quoted, 125
Ardennes Forest (Arduenna), 88, **88–89**
Ariovistus, 66, 68, 69, 74, **74**
Aristocrats, see Patricians
Arms and armor, 5, 8, **41, 58–59, 60,** 61, 62, **62,** 63, 64, **64,** 65, **65,** 69, 70, **70,** 71, **72–73,** 74, **74,** 79, **81,** 82, **89, 90–91,** 91, 98, **99, 134–135,** siege warfare, 24, **24,** 73, 86, 92, **92–93,** 94–97
Arsinoë, 120, 121, 130
Asia, 27, 28, 31, 53, 127, 128
Augustus (Octavian), 144, 148, **149**
Autun, 65, 66, 75, 96
Balearic Islands, 64
Belgium (Belgi), **84–85**
Besançon, 66, 68
Bibulus, 52, 55
Bithynia, 22
Black Sea, 19, 22
Bona Dea, see Caesar
Bourges, siege of, 92, **92–93,** 96–97
Brindisi (Brindisium), 109, 112, **112**
Britain, 64, 77, 78, **78,** 79, 80, 81, 89
Brutus, Decimus, 143
Brutus, Marcus, 140, 142, **142, 143,** 144, 147, **147,** 148
Caesar, Gaius Julius, cover, **6–7, 8, 39, 46, 57,** 80–81, **100–101, 102, 103, 107, 108–109, 130–131, 133** 135, 144–145, 146, 147, 148, 150 back cover
   birth, 11
   youth and education, 16–17
   made Priest of Jupiter, 21
   at siege of Mytilene, 22
   captured by pirates, 24, 26–27
   fights Mithridates, 27
   appointed to College of Priests, 37
   elected tribune, 37
   serves as quaestor in Spain, 40
   elected aedile, 42
   elected High Priest, 43
   heads popular party, 45–48
   elected praetor, 48
   Bona Dea scandal, 48–49, 59
   governor in Farther Spain, 52
   campaigns in Spain, 52
   elected consul, 52, 111, 125

   member of Triumvirate, 53–55
   governor in Gaul and Illyria, 58
   campaigns against Helvetii, 64–65
   campaigns against Germans, 66–69, 76–77
   campaigns against Belgae, 69–70
   defeats Nervii, 70–73
   defeats Atuatuci, 73
   campaigns against Veneti, 74–75
   invades Britain, 77–81
   puts down Gallic uprising, 81–89
   fights Ambiorix, 92
   fights Vercingetorix, 92
   besieges Bourges, 96–97
   takes Alesia, 98–99
   fights in civil war, 101–133
   crosses Rubicon, 106
   marches on Rome, 106–109
   campaigns in Spain, 111
   dictator of Rome, 111–112
   fights Pompey at Pharsalia, 112–114, 115
   campaigns in Egypt, 115–121
   aids Cleopatra, 119–121
   campaigns in Asia Minor, 122–124
   campaigns in Africa, 125–128
   honored in Rome 128–133
   last military campaign, 133
   becomes dictator of Rome, 133
   institutes reforms, 137–138
   assassination plot against, 140–144
   death, 6, 7, 11, 144, 147
   character, 6–7, 11, 21, 22, 24, 27, 37, 38, 40, 41, 43, 45, 46, 49, 52, 64–66, 71, 73, 77, 98, 112, 115, 119, 131, 133–134, 137, 140
   official acts, 55, 57–58, 73, 110, 111, 112, 125, 137–138
   political philosophy, 101, 103, 134–135
   quoted, 43, 78, 102, 124, 143, 144
Calendar, Roman, 137, 138, **138**
Calpurnia (Caesar's third wife), 55, 143, 144
Carrhae, 92
Casca, 144
Cassius, Gaius, 140, 144, 148
Cassivellaunus, king of Britons, 81
Castor and Pollux, Temple of, 14, **14,** 17
Catiline, 45, **45,** 46, 47, 59
Cato, 47, **47,** 48, 52, 55, 58, 59, 73, 77, 103, 125, 128
Catulus, 48
Cavalry, 64, 66, 70–71, **71,** 77, 79–80, 88, **89,** 91, 96, 98, 112, 116–117, 133, see also Roman armies
Cévennes (mountain range), 92
Chariots, 81, **81,** 129
   chariot races, **front endsheet,** 8, 35, **35**
Cherbourg peninsula, 74
Cicero, 23, 43, 45, **45,** 47–49, 55, **55,** 59, 109, 148
Cicero, Quintus (brother of Cicero), 86, 92
Cinna, 20–21
Civil War, 13, 105, 109, 112, 115–117, 133, 140
Cleopatra, 119, **119,** 120–121, **122–123,** 123, 130, **132,** 133, 138, 148

Coins, Roman, **title page,** 26, 27, 38, 112, **112, 131, 133,** 145, **145**
Coliseum, 16, **16**
College of Priests, 17, 27
Commentaries (Caesar), 78, 83, 97, see also *De Bello Gallico*
Commoners, see Plebians
Concord, Temple of, 14, **14–15,** 17
Copley, John Singleton, sketch by, **68–69**
Cornelia (Caesar's first wife), 21, 24, 40, 48
Cotta, Caius, 17, 27, 82, **82–83,** 83
Crassus, Marcus Licinius, 40–42, 47–48, 53, 55, **56,** 73–74, 89, 92, 138
Crassus, Publius (son of Marcus), 69, 74
Curia, 14, **14,** 16
Curio, 104–106, 111
Cyprus, 59, 73
De Bello Gallico (Caesar), 96–97, **96–97,** see also *Commentaries*
Dendera, Egypt, 121
De Republica (Cicero), 55, **55**
Dolabella, Gnaeus, 24
Donatello, sculpture by, **147**
Dumnorix, 80, 81
Dyrrachium, 113, 114
Egypt, 43, 64, 115, 119, **119,** 120, **120–121,** 121, 123, 130, 133
Egyptians, 115, 121, 138
Elections, Roman, see Roman government, chart of
Engineering, 64, **64,** 73, 77, **77,** 79, 96–98, 111, 137
Enipeus River, 116
Ferrero, Guglielmo, quoted, 38
Forum, 14, **14–15,** 16–18, 21, 37, 43, 48, 55
France, 58
Gaul, 47, 50–51, 61, 62, 64, 66, 69, 73–75, 77–79, 81, 89, 91, 92, 97, 99, 101, 103–105, 109, 128, 129, 143
Gauls, **57,** 58, **66–67,** 67–68, **68–69,** 71, **71, 72–73,** 73, 77, 78, 82, 86, **86, 87, 90,** 91, 92, 95–99, **99**
Geneva, 64
Gergovia, 98
Germany, 64, 77
Gladiators, 31, 34, **34,** 35, **36,** 37, 42, 47
Gleyres, Charles, painting by, **75**
Greeks, 24, 46
Hathor, Temple of, **120–121,** 121
Hercules, Temple of, 40
High Priest of Rome, 14, 17, 27, 43, 50–51
Ilerda, Spain, 111
Jerusalem, 127
Jews, 122, 127, **127**
Juba, king of Numidia, 12, 111, 125, 128, 130
Julia (Caesar's aunt) 11, 12, 38
Julia (Caesar's daughter) 24, 55, 89
Julian family, 11, 12, 21, 38
Jupiter, priest of, 21
Labienus, 65, 71, 96, 109, 125, 126, 133
de Landi, painting by, **122–123**
Legionaries, 62, **62,** 70, 71, 99, **99,** 117, 119, **119,** 127, **127,** 133

Legions, 63, 64, 69, 70, 73, 75, 77, 79, 80, 89, 98, 105, 117, 126, 127, 133
Lepidus, 111, 144
Loire River, 74
Luca, Italy, 73
Mantegna, paintings by, **134, 135**
Maps, **16, 20–21, 78, 84–85, 88–89, 124–125**
    of battles, **63, 82–83, 94–95, 113, 116–117, 128**
Marcellus, 105–106
Marius, Gaius, 11, 12, **12**, 13, 16, 18–21, 24, 38, 40, 46, 61, 66, 104
Marseilles, siege of, 111
Mediterranean, 20, **20**, 22, 26, **26–27**, 28, 46, **84–85**, 125, 128, 148
Metellus, Quintus, 12
Michelangelo, sculpture by, **143**
Mithridates, king of Pontus, 19, 20, **21**, 22, 24, 27, 122
Munda, Spain, 133
Mytilene, siege of, 22, **22**, 24
Narbonne, 92
Nepos, Metellus, 48
Nicomedes, king of Bithynia, 22
Nile River, 119, **119**, 121
    Caesar's cruise on, 121–122
Parthia, 138
Parthians, 89, 92, 143
Patrician party, 43, 45, 48, 52, 53, 92, 99
Patricians (aristocrats), 11, 16, 17, **17**, 21, 24, 28, 31, 37, 38, 45–47, **47**, 48, 49, **49**, 50–52, **52**, 61, 101, 105, 109, 135, 137, 140, 143
People's Assembly, 19, 43, 50–51, 55, 139
Pharnaces, 122, 124, 130
Pharos Island, 121
Pharsalia, battle of, 114, **114–115**, 115, 116–117, **116–117**, 128
Pirates, 22, 24, 26, **27**, 31, 43
Plebeians (commoners), 11, 12, 28, 31, 45, 48, 50–51, **52**, 61, 125, **136–137**, 137
Plutarch, 26, 147
    quoted, 26, 43
Pompeia (Caesar's second wife), 48–49
Pompeians, 128, 133
Pompeii, wall paintings from, **10, 29**, 49, **49**
Pompey (Gnaeus Pompeius), 37, **37**, 40, 41, 42, 46, 48, 53, 55, **57**, 73, 74, 89, 105, **105**, 106, **106**, 108, 109, 111–117, 140, 144
    quoted, 41
    sons of, 125–126, 133
Pontus, 19, 122
Popular party, 12, 21, 24, 46
Po River, 58
Provinces of Rome,
    Asia Minor, 19, 22, 24, 89, 122
    Cisalpine Gaul, 58, 69, 92, 105–106, 135, 139
    Farther Spain, 40, 111
    Greece, 19, 20, 40, 46, 62, 109, 112
    Illyria, 58, 74, 113
    Italy, 13, 21, 31, 40, 59, 65, 73, 91, 92, 105, 106, 109, 113, 121, 137, 148

Macedonia, 24
North Africa, 28, 125–128, 130
Sardinia, 111
Sicily, 28, 40, 111
Transalpine Gaul, 58, 59, 64, 92, 96
Ptolemy (geographer), map by, **20**
Ptolemy (ruler of Egypt) 119–121
    dynasty of, 121
Regia, 17
Rhine River, 66, 68, 69, 75, 76, 77, **84–85**
    bridge across, 77, **77**
Rhone River, 64
Roman armies, 8, 12, 13, 18, 19, 24, 27, 31, 41, 43, 47, 48, 53, 55, 58, **58**, 59, 60, **61, 63**, 65, 67, **67**, 68, **68–69**, 69, 70, 71, 74, 75, **75**, 77, 79, 81, 82, 86, 89, 92, 94–95, **94–95**, 96–98, **100–103**, 102, 104, 106, 108, 111–114, **114–115**, 116–117, **116–117**, 119–122, 124, 126, 128, 130, 133, 137, **back endsheet**
    history of, 61, 71
    organization of, 61, 63–64
    revolt of, 125
    rewarded by Caesar, 131
Roman Empire, 20, 28, 71, 99, 148
    map of, **124–125**
Roman government and politics, 8, 11, 12, 14, **14–15**, 16, 17, 20, 21, 23, **23**, 24, 27, 28, 31, 34, 37, **37**, 38, **38**, 40, 41, 42, **42**, 43, **43**, 45, **45**, 46–48, 52, 53, 58, 59, 73, 77, 89, 92, 101, 103–106, 108, 109, 111, 124, 125, 131, 133, 134, 137–139, **139**, 140, 143, 144
    chart of election system, 50–51, **50–51**
Roman life,
    art and architecture, **cover, 10**, 11, 12, **12, 13**, 14, **14–15**, 16, **17**, 18, 19, **23, 26–27**, 28, **28–29, 30, 31, 32–33, 34, 35, 36**, 38, **38, 39**, 46, **46, 47**, 48, **48, 49, 52–53, 55, 58–59, 66–67**, 71, **71, 73, 87, 104, 105, 107, 110, 111, 118, 119, 123, 126–127**, 129, **129**, 131, 133–134, **136–137**, 140, **140, 141, 148, back endsheet**
    business and economics, 17, **18–19**, 19, 21, 22, 26, **26–27**, 28, 37, **37**, 45, 46, 50–51, 80, 111, 112, 137
    customs and religion, 11, 16, 17, **17**, 18, 19, 21, 23, **23**, 28, **28–29**, 31, **31, 32–33**, 34, 37, 38, **38**, 43, **43**, 49, **52**, 58, **58**, 111, **111, 112**, 128–133, 140, 141, **141**, 148, *see also* Forum
    feasts and games, **front endsheet**, 31, 34, **34**, 35, **35**, 37, 42, 128–129, **129**, 130–133
Roman Republic, 71, 101, 106, 135, 148
Roman ships, 74, 75, 76, **76**, 77, 79, 80, **80–81**, 112–114, 131, 138
Romans, 16, 19, 21, 28, **28**, 31, 34, 40, 62, 63, 68, 69, 73, 77, 79, 82, 97, 111, 127, 130, 139–141, 143, 148
Rome, 6, **6**, 8, 13, **14–15**, 16, **16**, 18–22, 24, 26–28, 31, 37, 40, 41, 47,

48, 50–53, 58, 59, 61, 67, 73, 74, 77, 80, 89, 91, 92, 103–106, 108, 109, 111, 112, 120, 122–125, 128, 130, **130–131**, 133, 135, 137–140, 143, 148, 150, **back endsheet**
Rostra, 14, **14**, 17, 21
Rubens, drawing by, **146**
Rubicon River, 100, **100–103**, 102, 104, 106, 108, 109, 115
Sabinus, 82
Sambre River, 70
Saône River, 96
Saturn, Temple of, 14, **14**, 17, 48
Scipio, 114, 126
Senate, 6, 11, 12, 16, 19, 28, 37, **37**, 40–43, 45, **45**, 46–48, 50–51, **50–51**, 52, 53, 55, **56–57**, 58, 73, 103–106, 109, 125, 128, 139, 140, 143, 144
Senators, 16, 17, 47, 101, 109, 134, 140, 144
Slaves, 21, 28, **28–29**, 31, 67, 80, 86, 122
Social Wars, 19
Spain, 28, 40, 50–51, 106, 111, 128, 133, 139
Spartacus, 31, 41
Standard-bearers, 61, 79, 88, **89**
Standards, 61, **61**, 71, **75**, 80
Suetonius, 22, 102
    quoted, 22, 40, 132–133
Sulla, Lucius Cornelius, 13, **13**, 19–22, 24, 40, 41, 43, 46–48, 112
    quoted, 22, 46
Tabularium, 14, **15**, 18
Tenth Legion, 66, 79, 125
Thames River, 81
Thapsus, 126
    Battle of, 128, **128**
Thermus, Minucius, 22
Tiber River, 137
Tiepolo, painting by, **132**
Tribes,
    Aedui, 65, 80, 97, 98
    Aquitani, 78, **78**
    Atuatuci, 73
    Belgae, 69, 70, 75, 76, 78, **78**, 82, **88–89**
    British Celts, 78, 80
    Britons, 77, 79, **80–81**, 81
    Germans, 13, 59, 66, 68, 69, 75, 77, 82, **88–89**, 98
    Helvetii, 59, 64, 65, 66, 75, **75**
    Nervii, 70, 71, 73, 82, 86, 88, **88–89**
    Sequani, 66
    Spanish Celts, 78, 80
    Suebi, 76
    Veneti, 74, 75, 76
Triumvirate (first), 53, 55, **56–57**, 58, 69, 73, 74, 89
Triumvirate (second), 144, 148
Twentieth Legion, emblem of, **79**
Uccello, Paolo, 115
    paintings by, **6–7**
Utica, 128
Venus, **10**, 11
Vercingetorix, 92, 94–99, 130, **130**
Vesta, Temple of, 14, **14**, 17
Vestals, House of, 14, **14**, 17
Via Sacra, 14, 15
Weapons, *see* Arms and armor